The Mildenhall Treasure

K. S. Painter

The Mildenhall Treasure

Roman Silver from East Anglia

Published for
The Trustees of the British Museum
by
British Museum Publications Limited

Contents

List of Plates and Figures

All photographs were taken by Mr Peter Hayman of the British Museum's Photographic Studio.

New text-figures for this handbook have been drawn by Mr P. C. Compton, Senior Illustrator in the Department of Prehistoric and Romano-British Antiquities.

Preface

The Mildenhall Treasure is one of the major items in the collections of the Department of Prehistoric and Romano-British Antiquities in the British Museum. It was acquired by the Museum in 1946, and Mr J. W. Brailsford's illustrated handbook, describing all the objects in the hoard, was published in 1947. As well as a more recent edition of that handbook, published in 1955, many other discussions of the treasure have since appeared in print; in particular, the present author's paper 'The Mildenhall Treasure: A Reconsideration' (*The British Museum Quarterly*, vol. xxxvii (1973) reassessed the significance of this unique group of silverware, and sections from the text of it are incorporated here. This fuller and more detailed publication includes current scientific work (Appendix A, on the examination of the Great Dish by Mrs Janet Lang of the British Museum Research Laboratory) and a far larger number of drawings and photographs than have been published to date. The photographs, none of which has been published before, include details which give a good impression of the superb technical quality of the objects.

The discussion and conclusions owe much to the published work of Mr J. W. Brailsford, Professor J. M. C. Toynbee, Professor S. S. Frere and Professor D. E. Strong. The author would also like to thank his Departmental colleagues Mr P. C. Compton and Miss E. Bird. Above all, however, the preparation of this work for publication has been undertaken by Miss C. M. Johns, and I should like to pay a particular tribute to her ungrudging efforts and help.

K. S. Painter

Deputy Keeper
Department of Prehistoric and
Romano-British Antiquities

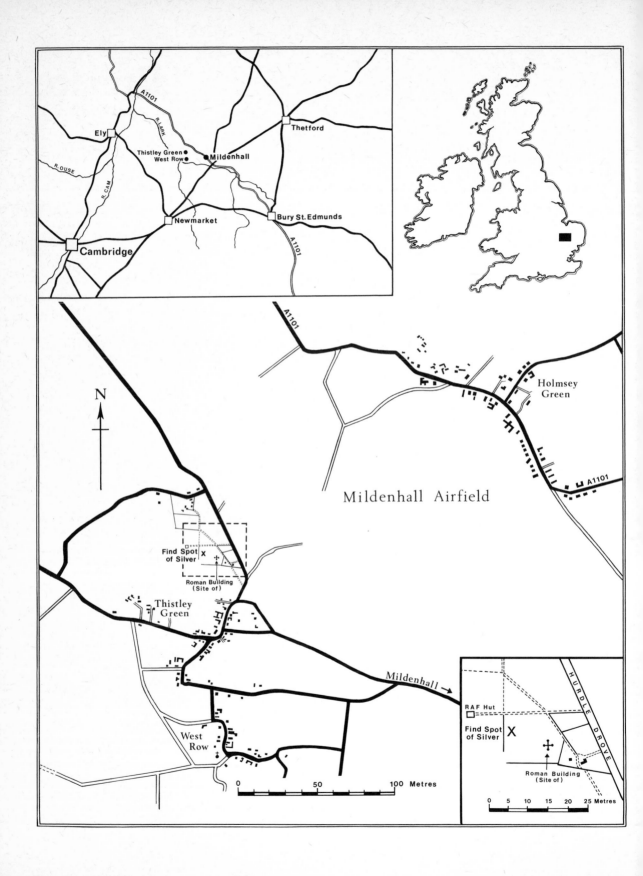

A1101

Ely
Thistley Green
West Row
Mildenhall
Thetford

R. LARK
R. OUSE
R. CAM

Newmarket
Bury St. Edmunds
A1101

Cambridge

N

A1101

Mildenhall Airfield

Holmsey Green

A1101

Find Spot of Silver
X
Roman Building (Site of)

Thistley Green

Mildenhall →

West Row

0   50   100 Metres

RAF Hut
Find Spot of Silver
X
Roman Building (Site of)

HURDLE DROVE

0 5 10 15 20 25 Metres

The Discovery of the Treasure

About 1942 a hoard of thirty-four Roman silver objects of the fourth century AD was found at West Row, on the edge of the Fens, near Mildenhall, Suffolk (Fig. 1). The hoard was discovered accidentally by Mr S. Ford and Mr G. Butcher while ploughing a field, and there are thought to be remains of a fourth-century building within thirty yards of the reported find-place of the treasure. At the official inquiry held in 1946 it was stated that the silver had actually been found four years earlier, the plough having been set to work four inches deeper than had formerly been the case; that the ploughman's employer, at first believing the articles to be of lead or pewter, had kept them in his house; and that the rich designs on the bowls and dishes had been completely obscured by incrustation when they were found, and were only gradually revealed by cleaning. On 1 July 1946, the Mildenhall silver was declared Treasure Trove, and consequently the property of the Crown. It was then acquired by the British Museum.

Its Date and Origin

The treasure may be divided into a number of component groups and single pieces, each distinguished by stylistic peculiarities. In seeking analogous pieces by which to assess the date of the treasure as a whole, it is necessary to treat these component elements separately.

The figures on the great dish and the two platters are naturalistic and almost purely classical in style. On silver-ware, however, the classical style could survive with very little alteration until very late, as, for instance, on the amphora and bucket from Conceşti, which probably date from the end of the fourth century AD.[1] Moreover, the borders of large beads and the low solid relief, with incised detail embodying certain definite conventions, are characteristic of the fourth century AD.[2] Our three Mildenhall pieces were undoubtedly made during that period. Certain details of the ornament support this dating. The *coiffure* of the maenad with the tambourine on the great dish, for instance, is a well-known fourth-century fashion, and a satyr on a flagon in the Traprain Treasure is strikingly similar to our examples.[3] The naturalism of the figure-ornament on the Mildenhall dish and platters can be matched on such well-known pieces as the Parabiago Patera, the Conceşti pieces, the Projecta casket from the Esquiline Treasure, the Corbridge lanx, the fourth-century Diana platter from Rome and a dish from Baku in the Caucasus which shows a Nereid riding a hippocamp surrounded by Tritons and Nereids.[4] Technically the last three are very similar to our dish and platters. The Mildenhall figures, however, seem livelier, and perhaps therefore earlier; consequently it may be that the manufacture of the great dish and platters is a little earlier in the century than that of the Corbridge lanx, which probably dates from the reign of Julian (AD 355-363), most probably *c.* AD 363.[5]

The geometric ornament of the niello dish (Catalogue no. 4) is very different from that on any other of the Mildenhall pieces. It has a central roundel with a complex geometric pattern of circles and squares and similar geometric and floral patterns on the broad, slightly raised, flange round the edge. The dish is edged with heavy beading. The ornament belongs to a style which, Kitzinger has suggested, reached its climax about AD 400.[6] Analogies from Traprain, and the heavily beaded rim, support a fourth-century dating for this piece also.[7] Elaborate use of gilt and niello is characteristic of the period, both for the floral geometric ornament and for figured scenes. Plainer dishes of the period were often monogrammed with the name of their owner in the niello and gilt technique. There were two sets of small dishes in the Esquiline Treasure of the late fourth century; four were round with moulded rims, and four had openwork borders, both of which had the monogram of Projecta in gilt and niello letters within a gilt and niello wreath.[8] A large round dish, perhaps *c.* AD 300, from the Tomb of the Queen with the Golden Mask at Kerch has a similar wreathed monogram in the centre and gilt and niello ornament on the rim.[9] Another large dish (no. 9) with geometric niello patterns on flange and medallion, like that from Mildenhall, was found at Kaiseraugst.[10] A somewhat later example of the same style and technique is the Anastasius dish found in the Sutton Hoo treasure, and a dish with a figured rim and geometric ornament in the centre was found with the remarkable late antique amphora discovered at Conceşti, Moldavia, Romania.[11] Like the Oceanus dish (i.e. the Great Dish) in the Mildenhall Treasure, the niello dish is large, 55·6 cm in diameter, and both, therefore, are larger than the types of the period earlier than the fourth century, even though in general design the dishes of the fourth and fifth centuries follow the fashions of the third century. Two dishes found near Cesena (Bolognese) Italy, are 62 and 63 cm in diameter, and the sizes of the large dishes in the Treasure of Traprain ranged from 45 to 60 cm.[12] Enormous serving dishes, as Strong points out, are shown on wall paintings of the period.[13]

The covered bowl (Catalogue nos. 11, 12) is very similar to three bowls from the Chaourse Treasure, which was probably deposited about AD 270, and probably constitutes a more or less complete *ministerium* of that century.[14] On the latter the flange ornament is executed in relief, but on the Mildenhall bowl it is incised and inlaid with niello. The cover might be a fourth-century product, for its foliate ornament is similar to that of the Mildenhall fluted bowl; but its relief frieze, although related to those on the four larger flanged bowls, is also related to those on the so-called 'Hemmoor' buckets, and so there would be no difficulty in placing the cover, too, in the third century AD.[15] The occurrence of foliate designs in hoards deposited relatively late—such as the Balline hoard of the late fourth or early fifth century— need not mean that individual pieces cannot be as early as the third century. The Mildenhall bowl and cover, therefore, may possibly not belong together because they do not fit well; but there is no strong reason to suggest that the lid is later than the fourth century, while the bowl may be one of the earliest pieces in the Mildenhall Treasure.

Bowls with broad flat rims are found as early as the end of the first century AD (Catalogue nos. 5–10), and so are mask-and-animal friezes such as occur on the larger Mildenhall flanged bowls (Catalogue nos. 5–8). The friezes are perhaps more characteristic, however, of the mid-second to mid-third centuries AD, as is the wave ornament decorating the bowls of the two smaller flanged bowls (Catalogue nos. 9, 10). The flange bordered by large beads is often stated to be a characteristic of the fourth century; but these other characteristics may perhaps push these bowls back to a slightly earlier date. Parallels to the relief decoration on the flanged bowls are to be found on similar pieces in the Carthage Treasure, generally dated about AD 400; but the date of manufacture of the flanged bowls in either treasure need not be later than has been suggested.

Close parallels to the scalloped or fluted bowl and its handles (Catalogue nos. 15–17) are to be found in the Esquiline Treasure from Rome and the Traprain Treasure from Scotland, and a similar bowl found in Romania has a control stamp of the fourth or fifth century.[16] The particular Mildenhall variation of this type is a shallow bowl of fairly large size, which has on the inside a series of alternate broad flutes with rounded ends and flat, straight-ended panels which are usually decorated with chased leaf-ornament. In the centre there is usually a roundel which is also richly decorated with chased or engraved ornament. Besides the Traprain examples a similar bowl was found at Weiden, near Cologne.[17] The bowl from Traprain has an engraved scene on its roundel, showing a Nereid riding on a sea-monster. The Mildenhall and Traprain bowls were both equipped with swing handles soldered on to the outside of the bowls by means of pear-shaped mounts. There was also a pair of handles ending in swans' heads in the Esquiline Treasure, and these very probably belonged to the scalloped bowl. There can be no doubt that this group, including, of course, the Mildenhall fluted bowl, belongs securely in the fourth century, and the same period can be assigned to the other bowls with close-set fluting on the outside. The Cleveland hoard contains a fine fluted bowl on a tall base ring typical of the period. Bowls with fluting on the inside were also common, the fluting being often combined with a central decoration. A bowl in the Kaiseraugst Treasure has a series of wide radial flutes around a central medallion; the medallion and the narrow horizontal rim are decorated with chased ornament. The bowl of very similar shape in the Sutton Hoo burial, which has a central medallion with a profile female head in relief, may not be much later than the Kaiseraugst example.

Silver drinking cups are not common in the late hoards but a number of new and attractive shapes are found. The shallow goblets on a stem and wide base plate seem to represent a type peculiar to the period. There were fragments of six such goblets from Traprain, and there is a pair of such goblets in the Mildenhall Treasure (Catalogue nos. 13, 14).[18] On the Mildenhall examples the baluster stem is enclosed by four bars of square section converging at top and bottom. It has been suggested that the wide base plates could be used as miniature dishes or stands, and they are, in fact, decorated with chased leaf ornament on the underside. A similar dual purpose had been served by the 'egg-cups' from the Campanian hoards of the first century AD.[19] The rims of the Mildenhall cups and the edges of the base plates are beaded, like so many other vessels of the period.[20] It is difficult to find parallels for the Traprain and Mildenhall goblets, but Curle pointed out that the goblets are probably merely such as were used in the ordinary service of the table in Roman households of the fourth century.[21] The only close surviving parallel example seems to be the stemmed cup from the hoard of pewter vessels from Appleshaw in Hampshire.[22]

The Mildenhall Treasure contains five small ladles with the handles cast in the form of dolphins and joined to the bowl with arms of attachment terminating in birds' heads (Catalogue nos. 18-26).[23] The bowls are similar in shape to the bowls of saucepans and are plain except for a series of turnings on the bottom of the inside. There is a number of such small ladles with horizontal handles in the late hoards. There is a similar ladle in the Traprain Treasure with the handle in the form of a dolphin holding the rim of the bowl in its mouth.[24] A series of seven little ladles in the Carthage Treasure have a shallower, rounded bowl, and there is a very similar ladle in the hoard from Canoscio and a pair with inscriptions on the panel from the Desana hoard in Turin. The Mildenhall spoons are similarly characteristic of their period by richer ornamental detail than their predecessors. One important detail is the elaborate ornamental treatment of the junction between bowl and handle. The curving arm joining stem and bowl was often continued with a scroll curving towards the bowl; in the late spoons this scroll is a normal feature and it is not infrequently converted into an animal head. The bowls of the spoons were now frequently decorated, especially on the inside, and the Mildenhall spoons conform with their floral patterns and their inscriptions, some of them Christian.

Many attempts have been made to establish the main centres of production of plate in this period. After the founding of Constantinople and the partitioning of the Empire, there were many capital centres—Rome, Constantinople, Antioch, Trier, Milan, Ravenna—and many centres where first-class silverware was turned out for members of the court and wealthy citizens. Any of these might be expected to have set fashions in this period but there are very few facts to aid the attribution of particular pieces. Some light is thrown on the problem by the stamps which occur on a few surviving vessels of the fourth and fifth centuries. It seems that silver plate was taken to be stamped with a guarantee of quality, usually after the piece had been formed but before it was decorated, to an office of the *argentarii Comitatenses*, a department of the *Comes Sacrarum Largitionum*.[25] Only five examples of this early period of the fourth and fifth centuries are known. One of these, which is a flanged bowl of the fifth century found in Syria and now in Berlin, was stamped in an eastern city, almost certainly Constantinople.[26] A second example on a small fluted bowl also has a seated Tyche figure to be compared with coins of Theodosius II and Valentinian III.[27] An important set of stamps on the Cesena dish cannot unfortunately be read or interpreted; but it seems likely to have survived above ground for a long time until it was buried near Cesena (Bolognese) at the time of the Gothic war between AD 538 and 553.[28] It is clear that many more examples of stamps must be found before any useful general conclusions can be drawn from these early stamps.

Only in the case of one type of silver plate can an attempt be made to divide surviving silver into broad centres of manufacture on grounds of style, and this division may or may not stand the test of time. In 1971 the British Museum acquired a fourth-century silver spoon found at Biddulph in Staffordshire, probably in the latter part of the nineteenth century, which represents the remains of a small hoard of silver hidden at the end of the fourth or the beginning of the fifth centuries AD.[29] The spoon is 19·4 cm long and the inside of the bowl is inscribed in double-stroke letters with the Chi-Rho monogram between alpha and omega. Such inscriptions, of course, are common on fourth-century spoons. What is unusual about the Biddulph inscription is that, whereas most inscriptions on spoons, as in the Mildenhall and Canoscio Treasures, seem to be stamped, the Biddulph inscription is apparently engraved, and it is engraved with double-stroke letters.[30] Only two other double-stroke Chi-Rho inscriptions on silver spoons appear to be known, one from Carthage and one from Hof Iben, near Mainz, and on both the letters are apparently not formed with a point but with a short straight stamp. This latter technique is the one used also for the inscriptions on the two small round dishes in the Carthage Treasure, on the Projecta casket, and the two sets of four dishes in the Esquiline Treasure, and apparently on one of the mounts from the coffin of St Paulinus in Trier.[31] The double-stroke technique, however, is common to all these pieces including the Biddulph spoon, no matter whether the tool used was a punch or a graver, and it is useful to compare them with the glasses with double-stroke inscriptions lately studied by Dr D. B. Harden.[32]

The glasses fall into two groups, (A) goblets, and (B–C) flasks and bowls.

The find-places, dates and probable place of manufacture are:

A. *Goblets*
1. Found 5 km east of Germa (ancient Gerama), Fezzan. Tripoli Museum. Third century AD. Made in Egypt.
2. Found at Berslin, 55 km east-south-east of Ljubljana, Yugoslavia. Kunsthistorisches Museum, Vienna. Third century AD. Probably made in Egypt.
3. Found in the same tomb as no. 1. Two fragments only. Tripoli Museum.
4. Probably from Egypt or the Sudan. Myers Museum, Eton College. Fourth century AD. Made in Egypt.
5. Found at Arminna West, Nubia. Cairo Museum. Fourth century AD. Made in Egypt.
6. Found at Gebel Khor, Abu Sinna, west of Kalabsha in Lower Nubia. Cairo Museum. Turn of third and fourth centuries AD. Made in Egypt.

B. *Flasks*
7. From eastern Mediterranean area. British Museum. Fourth century AD. Made in Asia Minor.
8. Found in Asia Minor. Private possession. Fourth century AD. Made in Asia Minor.

9. From eastern Mediterranean area. Present whereabouts unknown. Fourth century AD. Made in Asia Minor.

10. Found at Dinar (ancient Apamea Kibotos), south-west Asia Minor. R.G.M. Köln. Fourth century AD. Made in Asia Minor.

11. From eastern Mediterranean area. Marx Collection, Köln. Fourth century AD. Made in Asia Minor.

12. From eastern Mediterranean area. Present whereabouts unknown. Fourth century AD. Made in Asia Minor.

13. From eastern Mediterranean area. City Museum and Art Gallery, Birmingham. Fourth century AD. Made in Asia Minor.

C. *Bowls*

14. Found at Dinar, south-west Asia Minor. R.G.M. Köln. Fourth century AD. Made in Asia Minor.

15. Found on the site of the Apostelnkloster, Köln. R.G.M. Köln. Fourth century AD. Made in the Syro-Palestine area.

16. Found near Jerusalem. Dumbarton Oaks Museum, Washington. Fourth century AD. Made in the Syro-Palestine area.

All the glasses belong to the third or fourth century, making them contemporary with the metalwork which is our main concern. It is interesting that only one piece comes from the west, from Cologne, and leads to Dr Harden's conclusion on the unity of the group, despite the probably local manufacture of the Cologne piece: 'Is there any connection between the Egyptian, Asia Minor, Syro-Palestinian and (possibly) western examples, or are they to be ascribed to independent developments? Knowing the ease and determination with which glass-workers moved around in antiquity, it is, I believe, highly likely that some glass-cutter will have brought the idea of making double-line letters with him from Egypt—where it undoubtedly first arose—to other parts of the east, and even perhaps—himself or another to the west. That on the whole seems more probable than independent development of such a peculiar, and, one might almost say, unnecessary method of working; for the more normal single-line letter would do the work just as efficiently.' Applying these convincing conclusions to the metalwork, it may be suggested that the Biddulph, Hof Iben, Carthage and Esquiline silver may also have an Eastern Mediterranean origin. The argument may be carried further when the sarcophagus of Paulinus from Trier is considered, for this bishop was banished to Phrygia by Constantius for his Athanasian views and only returned to Trier as a corpse after his death in Asia Minor in AD 358. The mounts on his wooden coffin have been thought to be of local Rhenish work; but in view of the double-line inscription on one of them and its correspondence with the Biddulph silver and its parallels, the silver and the coffin with its Phrygian exile may perhaps be thought of as reinforcing the probability of each having an eastern origin. Conversely, the spoons stamped with single-line inscriptions may well have a western origin, particularly in view of the common use and occurrence of such objects.

Besides the spoons certain groups of presentation silver plate can be linked by inscriptions applied by their makers, especially if they are associated with stamped ingots made for presentation by the same silversmiths.[33]

Examples are:

1. Sirmium. Two ingots found at Eni Eri, near Svirkovo, in Bulgaria, were stamped of MAXIMV FA SIRMIS and of MAXIMI FA SIRMIS. This silversmith from Sirmium may also have

made the three fragmentary, silver largitio dishes dated by their inscriptions to Licinius' decennalia in AD 317.

2. Salodurum (now Solothurn, in the territory of the ancient Helvetii). One of the ingots from the Sabac area in Yugoslavia is stamped VA SALODVR, which could be expanded either to *Vasculari Salodurum* or to *Valerii Salodurani*, either of which refers to Salodurum.

3. Yugoslavia or Bulgaria. Six double-axe two-pound bars of silver found at Sabac in Yugoslavia bear the same signature, that of Flavius Nicanus, *vascularius*, as do the two plates made for Licinius' decennalia and discovered at Cervenbreg in north Bulgaria, and the plate from Srem in Yugoslavia.

4. Rome. For *Fabri Argentarii* from Rome see H. Dessau, *Inscriptiones Latinae Selectae* ii (1902), no. 6077 and II, ii (1906), no. 7696.

The attribution of surviving silver to centres of manufacture seems at present impossible except in the case of certain types of spoons and other vessels which seem to be attributable broadly to the western or to the eastern parts of the empire on the style of their types of inscription, those with double-line inscriptions coming probably from the east. Other centres of manufacture are known, and it is tempting to assign those dishes and bowls decorated with ornament of an easily recognizable kind to one, or a few, centres of manufacture. Most of the surviving pieces have been found in the west; but works in the same style are widely distributed. One dish from the Treasure of Kaiseraugst has a careful pointillé inscription giving the name of Euticius of Naissus (Niş), who is almost certainly its maker. The richly decorated Achilles dish from the Kaiseraugst Treasure is signed by its maker, Pausylypos of Thessalonike. Except in these cases, however, and a few others like that of Maximus of Sirmium and the others mentioned above in connection with ingots, largitio dishes and inscriptions, there is no firm evidence, and the widely differing opinions that have been held about the origin of such pieces as the Theodosius dish in Madrid illustrate how difficult it is to solve on any other evidence such problems as the origins of most pieces in the Mildenhall Treasure.[34]

Christianity, Ownership and the Date of Deposition

The outstanding vessel in the Mildenhall Treasure is the magnificent Great Dish, decorated with Oceanus, a marine *thiasos* and a Bacchic *thiasos*.[35] The Great Dish is one of a number of such picture dishes which have been found in late hoards; but the three sets of motifs which it displays all occur together so persistently on pagan funerary monuments, such as Bacchic and other sarcophagi, that it is hard to believe that the juxtaposition of the themes is merely decorative or purely fortuitous and has no inner, symbolic meaning. Oceanus recalls the situation, according to one version of other-world topography, of the Islands of the Blessed; the Nereids riding over the waves on sea-beasts could represent here, as on sarcophagi, the journey of souls across the ocean to the after-life; and the Bacchic revel-rout could, again as on sarcophagi, be an allegory of souls in bliss in paradise—worked out here in the terms of the well-known story of the drinking contest between Hercules and Bacchus. The splendid decoration as a whole suggests a carefully thought out ritual or religious purpose. The closest parallel to this famous late-Roman picture plate is the rectangular dish or *lanx* found in the River North Tyne near Corbridge in the eighteenth century, which seems to be the only survivor of quite a large hoard.[36] The dish is framed by a raised border decorated with a running scroll that encloses a relief scene showing a group of deities worshipped on the island of Delos. It has been suggested that the subject was chosen to commemorate the sacrifice offered to Apollo at Delos by Julian the Apostate in AD 363 and that the dish should be interpreted as a product of the pagan reaction against Christianity under that Emperor.

The Oceanus dish, then, is basically pagan, as are also the other platters and dishes. Of the eight spoons, by contrast, five are of special interest in view of their Christian inscriptions, from which it has been deduced that the person who deposited the Mildenhall hoard, or at least some members of that person's family, had embraced the Christian faith. Professor Toynbee has pointed out that it would have been completely normal for the owner, or owners, of the Christian spoons to preserve the great Oceanus dish, the Bacchic platters, and the bowls with Bacchic heads and Centaurs, for all their pagan content, whether as heirlooms of a pagan ancestry, for family reasons, or as treasures for aesthetic reasons. Such a person, or persons, might even have been able to regard such motifs as symbols of the Christian after-life, just as pagans would have taken them, not in a literal sense, but as symbols of the pagan after-life. Christian connections for pagan pieces are borne out incontrovertibly by the rectangular *lanx*, found at Risley Park in Derbyshire in 1729 and since lost.[37] The decoration, with hunting scenes, heads, etc., followed pagan traditions; but the inscription on the back—EXSVPERIVS EPISCOPVS ECCLESIAE BOGIENSI DEDIT—is indisputably Christian and records its dedication by Bishop Exsuperius to an unidentified church. Equally, owners who had embraced the Christian faith often had Chi-Rho monograms and other Christian symbols engraved on their silver though its decoration might be purely pagan in inspiration, like the silver in the Esquiline Treasure from Rome.

The argument usually advanced is that the Mildenhall Treasure is essentially pagan in character, but later came into the hands of a Christian owner. It depends, however, on interpreting the pagan scenes on the most arresting pieces in a Christian manner; on the Christian symbols on three of the spoons, and on inscriptions on two of the spoons—PAPITTEDO VIVAS and PASCENTIA VIVAS—which may or may not have Christian overtones. The arguments concerning some of the pieces of plate could have been carried further in support of Christianity, as Curle pointed out in his study of the Traprain silver.[38] First, the fluted dish:[39]

> The purpose for which such suspended dishes were used is a matter of doubt. The fashion apparently prevailed in Early Christian times of suspending silver vessels as ornaments from the arches of the *ciborium* in the churches and even in the bays between the columns of the nave and other parts of the building. The *Liber Pontificalis* mentions 64 chalices as suspended between the columns of the Vatican Basilica (Smith and Cheetham, *Dictionary of Christian Antiquities*, 1875, *s.v.* 'Chalice', p. 341), and such a practice may well have been derived from the earlier pagan temples. It has been suggested (Sir Martin Conway in *Proc. Soc. Ant. Lond.* xxx, 2nd ser., 1918, p. 84) that the hanging bowls in churches were in some cases used as convenient receptacles for chalices and other precious objects which it was desirable to keep out of the way of rough handling, and that with a similar end in view and for the further purpose of decoration bowls may have been also hung in private houses. The objection to this theory in the case of the Traprain Law dish is twofold. In the first place, had the vessel been intended to serve a decorative purpose while suspended from an arch or roof, it is unlikely that so much beautiful workmanship would have been lavished on the interior, while the exterior, which would alone have been in view, was left severely plain. In the second place, it would have been equally irrational to enrich the interior of a dish which was to be used only as a receptacle for objects that it was desired to put out of reach of rough usage, seeing that it would require to be suspended at an elevation probably above the level of the eye. The position of the scutcheons indicates a desire to afford the freest possible access to the interior, and the rich decoration suggests that the interior was intended to be seen. It is possible, therefore, that such a dish may have been meant to contain water or perfume into which the hands were dipped while it was held in suspension.

Second, the goblets:[40]

> The fact that possibly two at least of the objects in the [Traprain] hoard, the small flagon, no. 2, and the colum or strainer, no. 111, may have been employed in the service of the Eucharist, suggests the spoil of a religious establishment of some sort, and makes it possible that in these goblets we have some species of chalice in use in the Early Church. In early Christian representations of the Last Supper, however, or of altars whereon the sacred vessels are displayed, the chalice is invariably a large cup with two handles and a high base, more resembling in form the chalices of later medieval times which have descended from them. A typical example, dating from the fifth century, may be the vessel from Amiens, preserved in the British Museum (Dalton, *o.c.*, p. 132, no. 658). In the *Liber Pontificalis* chalices both of gold and silver are mentioned, weighing from one to 58 lbs. (Atchley, *Ordo Romanus Primus*, p. 24). They were of two sorts—large vessels in which the wine was consecrated, and smaller cups, *calices ministeriales*, which

contained the unconsecrated wine and into which a small quantity of the consecrated element was poured. The weight alone makes it evident that the Traprain goblets are not chalices such as are referred to in early records. It is noteworthy also that not only do no religious symbols appear on any of them, but that the three letters, CON, scratched on the only base which we have, is apparently the owner's name. The probability is, then, that these goblets are merely such as were used in the ordinary service of the table in Roman households of the fourth century; and although no other example of such a cup seems to have survived to our time, we can see something of the kind on one of the ivory panels in the back of the chair of St. Maximianus, of early sixth century date, in the Cathedral of Ravenna. The panel illustrates the supper at Cana, with Our Lord in the act of turning the water into wine. To the right of Our Lord is a figure of a man holding in his left hand a wine cup. The bowl is somewhat less than hemispherical and, as the stem is held between the thumb and first finger, there is an indication that the stem is thin and the cup light in weight. It is true that in the representation the cup seems somewhat thick, but allowance must be made for the material from which it is carved (Garrucci, *Storia della Arte Cristiana*, VI, tav. 418, no. 4). A representation of a similar goblet is shown on both sides of a pyx (Garrucci, *o.c.*, VI, tav. 439, no. 6), and depicting the incident of the cup found in Benjamin's sack in the Scripture narrative of Joseph and his brethren.[41]

Third, the spoons:[42]

(Of the nine spoons in the Traprain Treasure, two, nos. 97 and 98, are stamped with the Chi-Rho). It is a moot point whether spoons so distinguished have in reality been used in the service of the Church or no. In the Eastern Church, where ancient usage is persistent, the Communion in two kinds is distributed by the officiating priest by means of a small spoon. With this he draws from the chalice a small portion of the bread, which has been moistened in the wine, and transfers it to the mouth of the communicant who stands before him. Though the possibility that this practice prevailed at a remote period in the Western Church is obvious, there is now no evidence to that effect, and as early as A.D. 1054 it was affirmed by Cardinal Humbert of Silva Candida that it had never been in vogue in the Latin Church at all. On the other hand, Ducange, under the heading *Cochlear*, quotes texts in which spoon and paten are mentioned in association, and one of these actually states that Eucharistic loaves were placed in the paten with the spoon (in Cabrol, *Dictionnaire d'Archéologie Chrétienne*). At the present day in the Roman Catholic service a spoon is used in mixing the elements—the water and the wine. It may even be used for administering the communion to very young persons, and this particular practice is believed to be very ancient. The spoon, therefore, may very well have been employed in the service of the Eucharist in the Western Church in early times, but that the monogram on the bowl implies restriction to such use is doubtful. Its appearance and that of other religious emblems or representations have been ascribed to a desire of conforming strictly to the Apostolic injunction: 'Whether ye eat or drink, or whatsoever ye do, do all to the glory of God' (I Cor. X. 31: quoted by Ducange in Cabrol, *o.c.*, *s.v.* 'Cuiller', p. 3173). Or again, the presence of the monogram on a spoon of this period, the fourth century, may be due merely to the prevailing fashion of placing religious emblems on common objects, by no means necessarily connected with worship. An obvious instance of that practice is supplied by the casket of Projecta in the Esquiline Treasure, which bears not only the Christian monogram and a religious sentiment, but also a representation of the birth of Venus.[43]

Curle's arguments then, advanced some fifty years ago in relation to pieces in the Traprain Treasure which might have seemed to support a Christian use, apply equally to the parallel pieces in the Mildenhall Treasure. It is evident, that is to say, it is generally admitted, that the Mildenhall Treasure is pagan in character, but it is argued to have come later into the hands of a Christian owner. It is equally evident, however, that the reverse could also be the case. It is true that we know that a good deal of plate was being made for religious use in the fourth century, and from the time of Constantine churches were vastly enriched with precious vessels. Constantine himself gave a dish (*patera*) weighing 15 lbs, five *scyphi*, and four other vessels to the Basilica of SS Peter and Marcellinus.[44] A wide variety of vessels would be used in the churches; but only in the case of the treasure of twenty-four silver vessels found at Canoscio in Umbria has it been firmly suggested that a single treasure all belonged to a Christian church.[45] The essentially pagan character, however, of the great dish and platters of the Mildenhall Treasure is generally agreed, and it has been demonstrated that the fluted dish, the goblets, and the spoons by no means carry Christian significance of themselves quite apart from demonstrating any general Christian character of the Treasure itself. Further, special pagan significance may be attached to the four bowls (Catalogue nos. 5-8), which have medallions in their centres showing Alexander, Olympias (Alexander's mother), a hunter in combat with a bear, and an unidentified female head. These seven pieces are of particular significance in identifying the Mildenhall Treasure with the pagan aspects of the pagan-Christian controversy in the second half of the fourth century because their subject-matter matches so closely that of the so-called contorniates, coin-like medals.[46] In 1943 Professor Alföldi called attention to a large group of contorniates which seem to belong to the period between about AD 355-360 and 410.[47] Emphatically pagan in content, they served possibly as New Year's gifts and certainly, of course, as pagan propaganda. Among the subjects represented on the obverse may be mentioned: Alexander the Great and emperors of the past, especially Nero and Trajan; and on the reverse: scenes from the Alexander romance, the pagan religions, including the cults of Magna Mater, Attis, and Isis, classical mythology, Roman legends, the races and games in the circus.[48] Rare but interesting portrayals on the reverse are of Greek and especially Roman literary figures, such as Horace, Terence, Sallust, Apuleius, and Apollonius of Tyana. The comparative popularity of circus scenes can be explained by reaction to the Christian writers' consistent and unanimous condemnation of the games in all their forms and by Constantine's prohibition of gladiatorial shows in AD 326. Shows in fact continued throughout the century, and Constantius III himself was deeply impressed by the monuments of pagan Rome, when he visited the city for the first time in AD 357, as we know from Ammianus Marcellinus.[49] The historian tells us that the Emperor actually gave orders for the erection of an obelisk in the Circus, and the commemorative verses inscribed on that obelisk have come down to us.[50] Further, Julian himself reacted against the Christian teaching that he had received in childhood, including that against shows, and general toleration was proclaimed for all, pagans, Jews and Christians. His most controversial step was the edict forbidding Christians to teach literature in the schools. The edict is logical enough, as A. H. M. Jones pointed out.[51] A teacher must instruct his pupils in the content as well as the form of literature; a Christian cannot honestly expound pagan thought when he believes that the gods whom the classical authors worshipped are devils.

There are, therefore, good general reasons for associating positively the scenes portrayed on a large proportion of the fourth-century part of the Mildenhall Treasure with groups of objects such as the contorniates of which the earliest group belong to the period between about AD 355 and 360, and which continue to be produced until about AD 410. What may be of over-riding importance in this context is that on the back of each of the two smaller Bacchic platters (nos. 2, 3) is a graffito in Greek characters reading ευθηριον. This is the genitive of the name Eutherios.[52] The name does not appear to be attested before the fourth century, and its most distinguished bearer was the Armenian eunuch who served under Constantine and Constans and was *praepositus sacri cubiculi* under Julian in Gaul from AD 355 to 361.[53] As the plate is of superb quality and bears graffiti in Greek cursive script which can be assigned with some confidence to the fourth century AD, it is possible that this pair of magnificent platters, and perhaps the rest of the service, may once have belonged to this official during his time in Gaul. It may have been disposed of by him before he returned to Rome, and some subsequent owner then brought the plate into Britain.

Whatever the exact ownership of the hoard, it is clear that it represents a wealthy man's possessions, hurriedly buried in the province in times of desperate emergency and never again recovered. Detailed comparison of individual pieces makes it clear that there are numerous and striking points of resemblance between the Mildenhall Treasure and that from Traprain. Some of the comparable pieces in each may well be products of the same workshop. The Traprain analogies are particularly valuable, because the date of deposit of this hoard is securely fixed by the associated coins, the latest two being two of the emperor Honorius (AD 395–423), and the bulk of the component pieces were undoubtedly manufactured in the fourth century. A major difference, however, between the hoards on the one hand from Traprain in Scotland, Coleraine and Balline, Co. Limerick, in Ireland, Gross Bodungen in Germany, and Høstentrop in Denmark, and, on the other hand, from sites such as Mildenhall in Suffolk, Kaiseraugst in Switzerland, and Pietroasa in Romania, is that the first five consist of bullion, much of which is broken-up table silver, while the latter group of three hoards have their vessels virtually complete.[54] The Kaiseraugst hoard, which has even been argued to have been the property of Julian himself, must have been left in Kaiseraugst in AD 361.[55] The Mildenhall platters, and perhaps the rest of the hoard, must have been left in the West in or before AD 361, the year Julian, accompanied by Eutherios, was summoned to the East by Constantius II and met his end in a conflict with the Persians in AD 363.[56]

The exact date of the deposition of the Mildenhall Treasure cannot be known; but if it occurred at approximately the same date as that of the Kaiseraugst hoard a number of occasions suggest themselves.[57] Early in AD 360 the Scots, who were at this period still based on Ireland, and the Picts of central Scotland broke the terms which had been imposed on them, presumably by Constans, and began to lay waste the regions near the frontier.[58] In AD 365 there were successful attacks by Picts, Saxons, Scots and Attacotti, and late in AD 367 the position degenerated alarmingly. As a result of a *barbarica conspiratio* a concerted attack was made upon the province, and its united planning caused a military disaster in the province, which was only put right in AD 368 by the appointment of Theodosius, father of the man who was later to become the Emperor Theodosius I.

The deposition of the Mildenhall Treasure might have been connected with any of these events; but there are particular reasons for considering the first in detail. When the Scots from Ireland and the Picts from central Scotland began to lay waste the regions near the frontier, Julian, cousin of the Emperor Constantius II, was Caesar for the Gallic provinces. He hesitated to cross to Britain himself because of his other commitments, especially in mid-winter, but he dispatched Lupicinus, his *magister equitum per Gallias*, with four regiments of *comitatenses* in his place. Nothing is recorded of Lupicinus' achievements; but he is known to have been a competent general, and he was presumably successful in imposing terms, for he returned to Gaul within a few months. During the interval Julian had been hailed as Augustus by his troops, and some anxiety had been felt about the reaction of

Lupicinus to the news, if he heard it while still in control of the British garrison as well as his own force.[59] In the event, however, the precautions taken seem successfully to have kept him in ignorance until he set foot in Gaul and could be arrested. It may be, of course, that Lupicinus was instructed by Constantius II, the legitimate Augustus, to arrest Julian because of his attempt to seize the throne, for this is the version given by Julian in a manifesto of AD 361, written in Illyricum.[60] Whatever the exact nature of the situation, there is enough information to reconstruct a possible occasion for the hiding of the Mildenhall Treasure in AD 360. Lupicinus was an eminently suitable and experienced soldier, and his promotion to the British command marked him out in Julian's entourage more than sufficiently for him before his departure to be presented by Eutherius himself, Julian's confidant and *praepositus sacri cubiculi*, with what we know as the Mildenhall Treasure. While Lupicinus was in Britain, Julian was declared Augustus by his troops and now openly declared his paganism. Lupicinus, however, like Constantius II himself, was a Christian and in charge of a substantial force of troops—four regiments, Aeruli, Batavi and two of Moesiaci—and it may indeed be that Julian suspected Lupicinus would be loyal to Constantius and so kept him in ignorance of events until he could recall him and arrest him on his own at Boulogne.[61] Alternatively, Julian's account to the Athenians may be true. It may be a fact that Constantius, on learning of, or anticipating, Julian's bid for supremacy, entrusted Lupicinus and Gintonius, with the assistance of Paul, Gaudentius, Lucilianus and Florentius, to arrest Julian and Sallust and remove them from command of the troops in Gaul. In this case what followed would be that Julian managed to outwit Lupicinus and to arrest him as he landed.

In either case the arrest of Lupicinus in AD 360 and his fall from Julian's grace would have been more than enough cause for Lupicinus' family or entourage in Britain to entrust their most valuable possessions, the Mildenhall Treasure, to a safe place in Suffolk in case the regiments in Britain threw in their lot with Julian after the successful military *coup* in Gaul.[62] If this explanation of the Mildenhall Treasure were to be accepted, then it would after all be possible to interpret the silver as the unrecovered property of a Christian, not on the grounds of the composition of the hoard, but because Lupicinus, a Christian, may have been the original owner.

Catalogue of the Treasure

The order is that of the Museum registration number of the objects: the catalogue numbers used by Painter (*see* Bibliography) and Brailsford (*see* Bibliography) are also given, and there is a concordance of numbers in Appendix B.

All items are of silver.

1 The Great Dish

Reg. no. 1946.10-7.1 (Painter 1; Brailsford 1)
Diameter 60·5 cm, weight 8256 g.

The most striking piece in the treasure is the superb round dish with elaborate figured decoration in relief and fine engraving and a heavily beaded rim (Pl. 1). The central feature is a mask of a sea-god, Neptune or Oceanus; he has large, staring eyes, broad cheeks, a seaweed beard and four dolphins emerging from between the wild locks of his hair (Pl. 2). The rest of the decoration consists of two concentric zones of figure-scenes, separated from one another by a border of scallop shells. The inner frieze shows a sea-revel of Nereids with mythical sea-creatures (Pl. 3). The outer frieze, which is far broader, contains a Bacchic revel depicting in a vivid manner the triumph of Bacchus, the God of Wine, over Hercules. Bacchus stands naked, his long hair crowned with a diadem and his foot resting on the back of a panther. With his right hand he holds aloft a bunch of grapes, while a *thyrsus*, the Bacchic staff, is supported on his left arm (Pl. 4). A Silenus approaches with a wine-cup, and Hercules, dead-drunk, is only saved from collapse upon his lion-skin by two helpful young satyrs, one of whom supports him in front, while the other clasps him round the middle from behind (Pl. 5). The remainder of the frieze is peopled by Maenads, Satyrs and a bearded Pan (Pl. 6), all whirling in the dance, with a panther and various Bacchic objects in the field.

2 Platter

Reg. no. 1946.10-7.2 (Painter 2; Brailsford 2)
Diameter 18·8 cm, weight 539 g.

The pair of small silver platters in the treasure are decorated with Bacchic themes in the same style and technique as the Great Dish, and they may well have been produced in the same workshop. This one is adorned with Pan, holding a *pedum* and playing the *syrinx*, and a Maenad playing the double flute. In the field are a reclining water-nymph and a fawn or doe with a snake (Pl. 7, left). Some details of the decoration are engraved. On the back of the platter is the inscription ευθηριου. The rim is beaded.

3 Platter

Reg. no. 1946.10-7.3 (Painter 3; Brailsford 3)
Diameter 18·5 cm, weight 613 g.

The platter, which matches no. 2 above, is decorated with two dancing figures: a young satyr and a Maenad, the latter with a *thyrsus* and tambourine (Pl. 7, right). In the field are other Bacchic motifs—a cloth or skin filled with fruit and knotted to a *pedum*, a pair of cymbals, a covered bowl and a *syrinx*. The engraved details include borders of a delicate scroll pattern on the Maenad's garment (Pl. 8). As on the matching platter, there is a graffito, ευθηριου, on the back (Pl. 9).

4 Dish with Niello Decoration

Reg. no. 1946.10-7.4 (Painter 10; Brailsford 4)
Diameter 55·6 cm, weight 5023 g.

This large silver dish has a broad flat rim, edged with large beads (Pl. 10). The rim and a circular medallion in the centre are decorated with incised patterns inlaid with niello (silver sulphide), giving a black linear design on the silver background. The designs are basically geometric, but include plant-derived rosettes and scrolls (Pls. 11–14).

5 Flanged bowl

Reg. no. 1946.10-7.5 (Painter 6; Brailsford 7)
Diameter 30 cm, height 9·6 cm, weight 1718 g.

This bowl is the largest of four in the treasure which have broad flat rims or flanges decorated with figured scenes in relief, beads around the edge of the rim, and a relief-decorated medallion in the centre (Pl. 15, right). The rim ornament, divided into four sections by large profile heads, includes bulls, boars, leopards, goats, sheep and griffins; the centre medallion shows a hunter attacking a bear (Pl. 16). On the underside of the flange are two inscriptions (Pl. 17 and Fig. 2), one of which, in scratched lines, may be a proverb, while the other, which is dotted, probably gives the weight of the vessel.

6 Flanged bowl

Reg. no. 1946.10-7.6 (Painter 7; Brailsford 8)
Diameter 26·8 cm, height 8·6 cm, weight 1271 g.

A bowl of the same form as no. 5 above (Pl. 15, left). The decoration on the rim is of animals and human heads, while the centre medallion bears a profile head of a young woman (Pl. 18). On the underside of the flange is a dotted inscription, probably giving a weight (Pl. 19). It reads
PXXΛII Ƨ II8ΛII

7 Flanged bowl

Reg. no. 1946.10-7.7 (Painter 9; Brailsford 10)
Diameter 26·8 cm, height 8·6 cm, weight 1301 g.

The third flanged bowl has a similar animal frieze round the rim as the bowls described above; the animals are goats, sheep, deer and a bear (Pl. 20). In the centre medallion is a male head, wearing a helmet (Pl. 22). The head probably represents Alexander the Great.

2 Flanged bowl, *Catalogue no. 5.* Inscriptions on the underside of the flange

8 Flanged bowl

Reg. no. 1946.10-7.8 (Painter 8; Brailsford 9)
Diameter 26·8 cm, height 8·6 cm, weight 1320 g.

This bowl closely matches no. 7 above, though the animal frieze has rather more variety, consisting of bears, deer, horses, leopards, a bull and boars (Pl. 20, left). The head in the centre of the bowl is that of a woman, but, unlike the profile on no. 6 above, the head is draped (Pl. 21). The woman is probably intended as Olympias, mother of Alexander the Great.

9 Flanged bowl

Reg. no. 1946.10-7.9 (Painter 11; Brailsford 11)
Diameter 16·8 cm, height 5·8 cm, weight 615 g.

This vessel forms a pair with no. 10 below; it is of similar form to the four larger flanged bowls, and has a beaded rim (Pl. 23, left). The rim is richly decorated with a vine-scroll containing leaves, flowers, grapes, birds and rabbits (Pl. 24 and Fig. 3). The interior of the bowl is decorated with shallow, curved flutings, and there is a central rosette motif with sixteen petals, surrounded by a double-beaded circle. On the base of the bowl is a scratched inscription, probably giving the weight (Fig. 4).

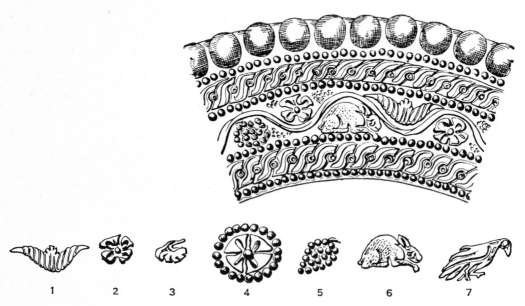

3 Flanged bowl, *Catalogue no. 9.* Detail of rim and the individual decorative motifs

4 Flanged bowl, *Catalogue no. 9*
Inscription on the base

10 Flanged bowl

Reg. no. 1946.10-7.10 (Painter 12; Brailsford 12)
Diameter 16·8 cm, height 5·8 cm, weight 627 g.

The matching vessel to no. 9, this piece has slightly more elaborate decoration on the rim (Pl. 23, right, and Pl. 25); the additional motifs are illustrated in Fig. 5. There is a graffito on the base similar to that on no. 9 (Fig. 6).

11, 12 Bowl with cover

Reg. nos. 1946.10-7.11, 12 (Painter 4, 5; Brailsford 5, 6)
Diameter 23 cm, height (together) 19·1 cm, weight (bowl) 1013 g., (lid) 840 g.

A flanged bowl with a high, domed cover which was probably not originally made for it (Pls. 26–28). The flange of the bowl has an incised foliate scroll originally inlaid with niello, and a bead-and-reel border at the edge. Within the bowl is an incised design of eight radiating leaves. The upper part of the cover bears a stylized leaf pattern, executed in broad shallow grooves, while the lower has a frieze of animals and profile heads in relief, with engraved details. Serving as a knob is a small silver-gilt statuette of a youthful triton sitting blowing a conch shell. This was not the original knob or handle.

13, 14 Pair of goblets

Reg. nos. 1946.10-7.13, 14 (Painter 14, 15; Brailsford 16, 17)
Diameter (bowl) 9·7 cm, (base) 11·5 cm, height 11·7 cm, weight, no. 13, 391 g., no. 14, 383 g.

A closely matching pair of shallow goblets with beaded rims (Pl. 29). The stems have baluster mouldings enclosed by four decorated square-sectioned rods which bow outwards, and have foliate terminals above and below. The bases of the goblets have beaded rims, and are decorated with a foliate pattern on the underside, so that the goblets could have been reversed to form small pedestalled platters (Pl. 30).

15-17 Fluted bowl with handles

Reg. nos. 1946.10-7.15-17 (Painter 13; Brailsford 13-15)
Diameter 40·8 cm, height 11·1 cm, weight 1575 g.

A large bowl with two swing handles (Pls. 31, 32). The vessel is fluted, with radial panels which are alternately flat and concave. There is foliate decoration on the flat panels, seven arranged on undulating stems, and the alternate seven on straight ones. A central panel contains a six-petalled rosette at the centre of a star formed of two interlocking triangles. The handles have leaf-shaped attachments and swan's-head terminals; they were originally soldered, not riveted, to the bowl, but were detached when found.

8   9   10   11   12   13   14   15

5 Flanged bowl, *Catalogue no. 10.* Motifs in the rim decoration additional to those on *Catalogue no. 9*

6 Flanged bowl, *Catalogue no. 10* Inscription on base

18-26 Five ladle-bowls and four ladle-handles

Reg. nos. 1946.10-7.18-26 (Painter 16-24; Brailsford 18-26)
Diameter of bowls, 5·7 cm, length of complete handles, 9·5 cm, weight of bowls 35-46 g., weight of handles 36 g.

The ladles were originally soldered to the cast dolphin handles (Pl. 33). The bowls are of hemispherical form, with thickened rims and concentric grooves on the base, resembling miniature Roman *paterae* (dishes). The handles are silver-gilt, and are cast in the shape of a dolphin. They have crescentic attachments for fitting to the rims of the bowls. The bodies of the dolphins have incised and dotted details, and the eyes were inlaid with a substance which is now lost (Pl. 34).

27 Inscribed spoon

Reg. no. 1946.10-7.27 (Painter 26; Brailsford 28)
Length 18·8 cm, weight 25 g.

Silver spoon with a pear-shaped bowl, inscribed PASCENTIA VIVAS (Pl. 35, lower, and Fig. 7). The handle is plain and tapering; it is of square section with bevelled edges, and is attached to the bowl by an openwork scroll.

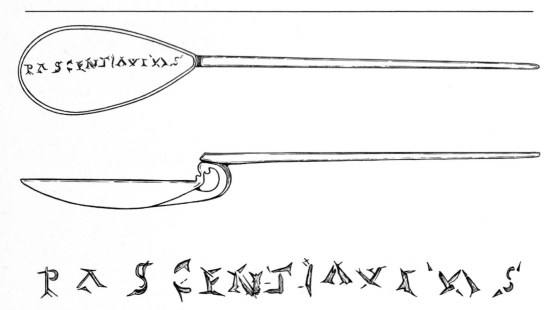

7 Spoon with the inscription PASCENTIA VIVAS. *Catalogue no. 27*

28 Inscribed spoon

Reg. no. 1946.10-7.28 (Painter 25; Brailsford 27)
Length 18·6 cm, weight 25 g.

A spoon with an oval bowl, within which is the inscription PAPITTEDO VIVAS in lettering clearer and neater than that on no. 27 above. (Pl. 35, upper, and Fig. 8). The handle is twisted at the end nearer the bowl, but has a plain, tapering tip. It is joined to the bowl by an openwork scroll.

29-31 Three spoons with Chi-Rho monograms

Reg. nos. 1946.10-7.29-31 (Painter 28, 29, 27; Brailsford 30, 31, 29)
Length (29) 20·1 cm, (30) 20·6 cm, (31) 20·4 cm; weight (29) 27 g., (30) 35 g., (31) 25 g.

Three closely similar spoons (Pl. 36 and Figs. 9-11), with pear-shaped bowls, plain tapering handles and openwork scroll attachments. Each has an inscription within the bowl, consisting of the Chi-Rho monogram between alpha and omega.

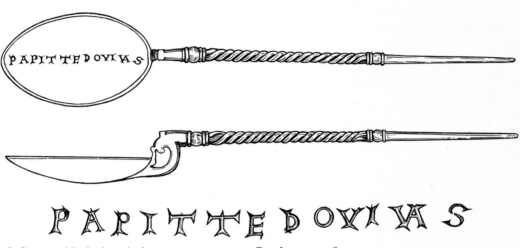

8 Spoon with the inscription PAPITTEDO VIVAS. *Catalogue no. 28*

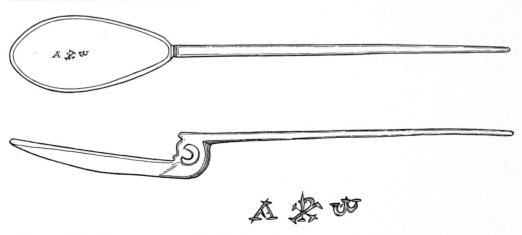

9 Spoon with Chi-Rho monogram. *Catalogue no. 29*

32-34 Three decorated spoons

Reg. nos. 1946.10-7.32-34 (Painter 32, 31, 30;
Brailsford 34, 33, 32)
Length (32) 16·7 cm, (33) 16·3 cm, (34) 17·2 cm;
weight (32) 20 g., (33) 17 g., (34) 18 g.

Three spoons, all with pear-shaped bowls, plain tapering handles and scroll attachments between handle and bowl (Pl. 37 and Figs. 12–14). All have foliate decoration within the bowl; on no. 32, the leaves are based on an undulating stem, while on the other two spoons, the stem is straight. This decoration is very similar to that on the large fluted bowl (nos. 15–17 above).

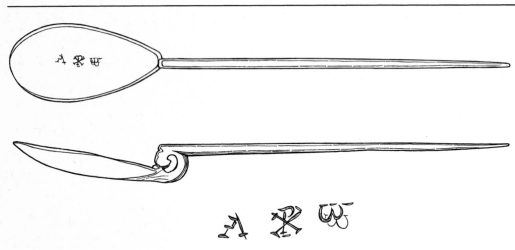

10 Spoon with Chi-Rho monogram. *Catalogue no. 30*

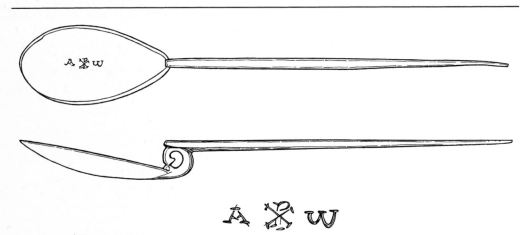

11 Spoon with Chi-Rho monogram. *Catalogue no. 31*

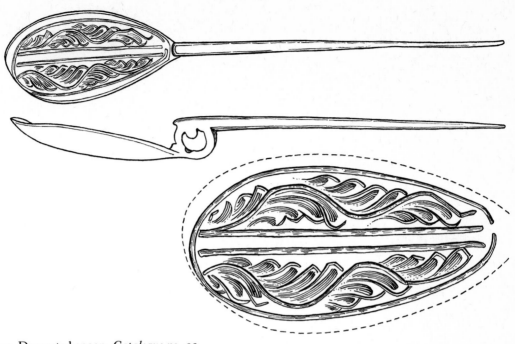

12 Decorated spoon. *Catalogue no. 32*

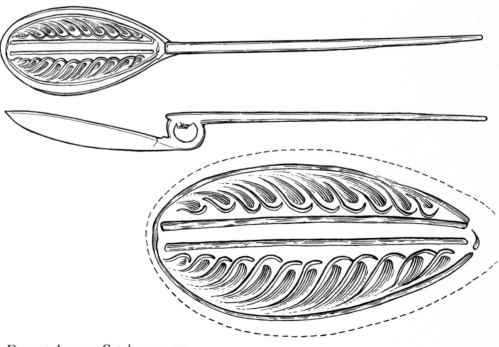

13 Decorated spoon. *Catalogue no. 33*

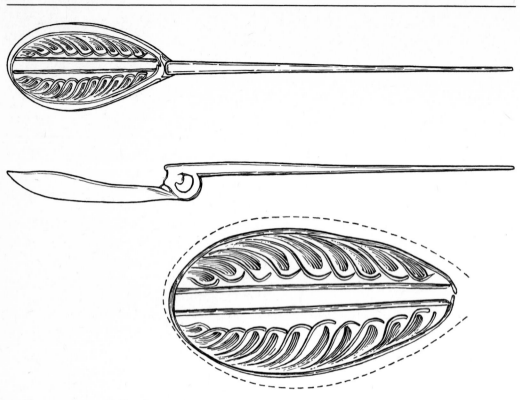

14 Decorated spoon. *Catalogue no. 34*

Appendix A
The Scientific Examination of the Great Dish

Introduction

After their acquisition by the British Museum in 1946, the objects in the Mildenhall Treasure were scientifically examined by Herbert Maryon, who published his main conclusions in two papers in *Man*.[63] Maryon's conclusions were based on a thorough physical examination of the dish and other objects in the hoard, but no samples were taken. He concluded first that the Neptune dish had not been cast; secondly, that the design had been executed by modelling and chasing from the front while resting on a steel anvil and that this was followed by scraping; thirdly, that the foot ring had been hard soldered onto the dish, and, fourthly, that the beaded decoration on the rim had been made by driving the metal into a square-faced punch with a hemispherical cup in the centre. Maryon's conclusions have not always been completely accepted: for example, it has been suggested that the design was carved rather than modelled and chased. It was therefore decided that the dish could usefully be re-examined using the techniques of metallography, scanning electron microscopy, X-ray fluorescence analysis and atomic absorption analysis. Maryon's conclusions could then be reassessed. This report does not consider the beading, discussion and conclusions on this, however, will appear in a later report when more detailed work has been carried out on comparable beaded material.

Technical Examination

The technical examination consisted of a physical examination using optical and scanning electron microscopy and an analytical examination, using X-ray fluorescence and atomic absorption analysis techniques.

1 Microscopy examination. Three small samples were obtained, one from the edge of a hole in the main part of the dish, one from the rim and a tiny fragment of folded-in metal from the back surface. These samples were mounted in thermal setting resin and were polished, etched and examined. All three showed worked and annealed structures, with intercrystalline corrosion visible close to the surface. Grain growth had taken place, and there was some liquation at the grain boundaries, particularly in the samples from the front and back of the dish. The latter two samples also showed signs of melting at the surface and some oxidation of copper within the metal to cuprite, which appears red in polarized light. Intercrystalline corrosion was visible under the surface layer in some areas, indicating that liquation and oxidation took place after corrosion. The sample taken from the rim did not appear to have been as severely worked as the other two, although this might be the result of a particularly thorough anneal.

2 Analytical examination. Most of the analyses were carried out using the X-ray fluorescence technique since this is a non-destructive method, requiring only that a small area of surface should be cleaned. The atomic absorption spectroscopy method, which requires small drilled samples of one to six milligrams was used to cross check the X-ray fluorescence results.

(i) *X-ray fluorescence.* In all, eight areas were examined by XRF, the surface layer being removed in each case by scraping with a jeweller's knife. Copper and silver were determined in each case, being the average of two determinations, the calculation procedure assuming a binary alloy. Three of these areas were later re-examined. The surfaces were re-scraped until constant results were obtained within the limits

35

of experimental error. In this case the minor constituents, gold and lead, were determined also, thus giving a complete analysis. In all cases the X-ray tube was used as a primary source and set at 20 KV, 0·6 MA with a counting time of 100 secs. Only four elements were found to be detectable above background levels, silver, copper, gold and lead. The accuracy of the XRF figures is about ±0·5% absolute for silver and copper and ±50% relative for minor elements. There does not seem to have been any significant change on rescraping. In the earlier set of results gold and lead were not analysed, so that the silver totals are higher than in the later analyses, where gold and lead were measured. (The analyses totals are assumed to be 100%.)

Table 1   X-Ray Fluorescence Analyses

Area	Element	First Analysis	Later Analysis
MILD 1 (rim)	% Ag	97·1	
	% Cu	2·9	
MILD 2 (rim)	% Ag	97·4	96·4
	% Cu	2·6	2·65
	% Au	n.d.	0·8
	% Pb	n.d.	0·2
MILD 3 (back)	% Ag	97·5	
	% Cu	2·5	
MILD 4 (back)	% Ag	97·3	97·1
	% Cu	2·7	2·55
	% Au	n.d.	0·4
	% Pb	n.d.	<0·1
MILD 5 (base)	% Ag	97·3	
	% Cu	2·7	
MILD 6 (base)	% Ag	97·1	96·7
	% Cu	2·9	2·5
	% Au	n.d.	0·5
	% Pb	n.d.	0·3
MILD 7 (base)	% Ag	97·0	
	% Cu	3·0	
MILD 8 (rim)	% Ag	97·6	
	% Cu	2·7	

(ii) *Atomic absorption*. For atomic absorption analysis samples were taken from two places by drilling, the base ring and the rim of the dish and one place by scraping, the back of the main body of the dish. The latter sample weighed only 1 mg as opposed to 6 mg for each of the drilled samples so that it was only possible to measure the major elements (copper and silver). Atomic absorption gives results which are accurate from 1% to 2% for major elements (Ag, Cu) and from 5% to 10% for minor elements. The method is discussed in more detail by Hughes, Cowell and Craddock (*Archaeometry*, 18, no. 1 (1976), pp. 19–37).

Table II   Atomic Absorption Analyses

Area	% Ag	% Cu	% Pb	% Au	% Bi	% Sn	Total
Base ring	97·2	2·5	0·39	0·85	0·06	<0·3	101
Rim	97·2	2·6	0·42	0·72	0·06	<0·3	101
Body	97	3·1	—	—	—	<0·3	

Table III

Comparison of X-Ray Fluorescence and Atomic Absorption Analyses
(Mean values for all areas analysed)

Element	XRF	AAS
% Ag	96·7	97·2
% Cu	2·55	2·55
% Au	0·6	0·8
% Pb	0·2	0·4
% Bi	—	0·06
Total	100·05	101·01

Physical Examination and Discussion
Four main points of interest were considered in relation to the Neptune dish. These were:

1   the construction of the dish
2   the execution of the design
3   the surface finish
4   the use of soldering and the foot ring

1 The construction of the dish. There are two main methods by which a large dish such as the Neptune dish can be made. The first method is to cast it, with or without the decorative design in the mould. The second method is to raise it either from a blank which might itself have been directly produced by casting or from an ingot containing a suitable volume of metal. The evidence suggests that it was raised from a cast blank.

The three microsections showed worked and annealed structures, indicating that the dish could not have been cast without subsequent working and heating processes being carried out. Examination of the surfaces of the dish, particularly the back, showed some casting fins which had been hammered into the surface of the metal. These may have been visible originally or revealed as a result of corrosion during burial. Near the centre of the dish on the underside there is an irregularly shaped shallow cavity which is clearly not a raising pip. It is suggested that this was the remains of a riser or a feeder used in the original casting process, where gases trapped during solidification left a cavity. Since raising is usually started from the centre and the silversmith works outwards to the rim in a spiral, the centre is often scarcely deformed, and a raising pip, or in this case a casting cavity, may remain undisturbed throughout the process. Hammer marks are visible near this cavity.

On the front and back surfaces there are small roughened areas which could be taken possibly as dendrites revealed by the action of corrosion during burial. Dendrites are branched tree-like structures which are the natural mode of solidification for most cast metals, exceptions being eutectics (where particular proportions of alloying elements are involved) and very pure metals. A replica of the areas on the dish, examined in the SEM, confirmed Maryon's opinion that they were merely pits caused by corrosion during burial. No dendrites were visible at low or high magnification. In fact a dendritic macro-structure, which can be seen with the naked eye or at magnifications of up to 10 or 20 times the original, can be retained even when the micro-structure shows that considerable working, accompanied by heat treatment, has been carried out. The metal varies in thickness, being fairly thick at the centre and thinning out towards the rim, which is indicative of raising. The casting fins and cavity at the centre suggest that the dish was cast to a suitable shape, while the worked and annealed micro-structure, the fact that no dendrites remain, the hammer marks and the variation in thickness show that the original casting was extensively worked to increase the over all diameter and shape the dish.

The rim itself is very much thicker than the body of the disc which is very thin near the rim. Thickening could have been achieved by (a) soldering on a rim; (b) casting on extra metal; (c) working down the centre of a disc of suitable dimensions to leave a rim of nearly untouched metal; (d) folding over the thinned edge a number of times and welding the layers with heat and pressure, or (e) tapping the periphery of the dish edge-on with a raising hammer. No traces of solder were found (a), and the extreme thinness of the adjacent metal at this point would have made soldering or casting on (b), a very difficult task indeed. Working the centre only (c) was a technique used on objects from the Traprain hoard, but is only suitable where a deep cup is to be produced. A folded edge (d) would have produced a laminated structure but a replica of a fractured surface (which gave a cross-section) failed to show laminations, and it is therefore likely that the edge was thickened by beating edge-on (e), a standard raising technique known as caulking.

2 The execution of the design. A design in relief, such as that on the dish, can be produced in a number of ways. These include:

(i) casting as part of the original mould;

(ii) applying suitably shaped pieces of metal, attached to the base by grooves cut into the surface being decorated, and fixed in position with solder or by burnishing over the edges of the join;

(iii) carving down the surface, leaving the figures in relief;

(iv) raising the relief parts of the figures from the back, perhaps finishing by chasing and a little punching on the front;

(v) working entirely from the front, either (a) punching down the background with metal mounted on a soft material such as pitch, or (b) displacing metal sideways while held on an anvil or hard surface.

As the dish was not cast to shape (see 1 above) the first suggestion (i) can be dismissed. The appliqué technique, often found in silver objects from Persia is readily revealed by a combination of physical examination and radiography, but in this case no joins were found at the edges of the figures.

The carving technique (iii), would leave a smooth back surface on the dish, and possibly a sharply 'layered' profile on the figures. In fact there were shallow hollows under the figures, not indicative of carving. The figures showed a series of 'layers' but the profiles were rounded, as though they had been in contact with a punch, rather than a cutting tool which would be necessary for carving.

If the figures had been raised from the back (iv), signs of hammering or punching on the back surface of the dish should be seen, a fairly thin silver would be used, and there would be hollows under the figures. In fact there was no sign of concentrated working on the back surface, the silver varied from thick to thin and the hollows under the figures were shallow and all rather similar, their appearance being unrelated to the thickness of the metal. It seems unlikely that the dish was raised from the back.

It seems most likely that the figures were raised from the front (v), being finished by chasing and punching. As Maryon pointed out, if the metal is mounted on pitch and worked from the front (va), the underside of the design is rounded and the metal surface smooth, with little or no bruising. If, however, the metal is held on an anvil or hard surface an imprint of the surface on which it was worked is visible. Maryon worked a sampler to demonstrate these effects, unfortunately no longer extant, but a new sampler was made by Chris Wheatley working with punches from the front with the silver resting on an anvil. This showed quite clearly the characteristics described by Maryon, the area under the figure was slightly hollowed, the back surface was somewhat bruised and its texture was roughened. The hollowing, bruising and texture on the sampler closely resembled those of the central disc within the foot ring on the Neptune dish. It seems likely therefore that Maryon's lateral displacement technique with the dish held on an anvil or hard surface was the method used to raise the figures.

3 **The surface finish.** Since the dish has been very extensively cleaned and treated since its removal from the soil it is difficult to know what the original surface was like. Curle suggested in his work on the Traprain hoard that a dull surface was preferred, but there is not sufficient evidence yet from unconserved objects to be sure of this.

Recently examined objects from the Water Newton hoard had polished rather than dull surfaces, but the quality of the polish was not particularly good, and many turning lines were visible because of the use of the lathe. According to Pliny fashions varied: 'Fashion in silver plate undergoes marvellous variations owing to the vagaries of human taste, no kind of workmanship remaining long in favour. At one time Furnian plate is in demand, at another Clodian, at another Gratian . . . at another time the demand is for embossed plate and rough surfaces, where the metal has been cut out along the painted lines of the designs . . . and other pieces of plate we decorate with filigree so that the file may have wasted as much silver as possible'.[64]

The figures on the Neptune dish are highly polished while the background on the front surface, the rim, the foot ring and the back surface of the dish have been scraped. The lines on the rim, foot ring and back surface are shallow, being between 1 μm and 100 μm wide and 0.05 μm to 50 μm in depth and are parallel over considerable lengths. The lathe was in use at this period in the Roman world, both for cutting metal away (turning)[65] and also for scraping the surface to remove any obvious bumps or asperities produced during raising.

The presence of an unscraped area at the centre of the underside of the Neptune dish, bounded by a scribed circle, is indicative of the use of a lathe, since the dish would be held in position by a chuck, probably made of wood, and the metal underneath this would remain unscraped unless treated by hand. Judging by the regularity of the grooves and their distance apart, a lathe was probably used for scraping the rim, foot ring and back surface of the Neptune dish. (A number of the bowls in the Water Newton hoard were quite clearly scraped in this way.) The front surface of the Neptune dish had also been scraped, but only between the figures; the lines ended at the raised figures and did not disappear beneath them, nor were they distorted, bruised or bent in any way as they would have been if the scraping had been carried out before the figures were raised. Scraped lines do not appear on the surfaces of the figures, indicating that the scraping was not the result of a final mechanical polishing process carried out either before or after excavation.

Liquation had been observed at the grain boundaries of the mounted specimens, and an examination of the back surface of the dish at low magnification showed that liquation had taken place quite extensively. This means that the dish was heated to such a temperature that the grain boundaries, which usually contain lower melting point components, become liquid. The specimen taken from the back of the dish showed oxidation of copper and had the appearance typical of fire stained silver. The oxidation occurs when the metal is heated in an open furnace or with a torch in an unrestricted atmosphere for too long. It is avoided as far as possible by silversmiths because the appearance of the silver is spoiled and the affected layer of metal must be physically removed to restore the colour which means loss of metal, patient work and repolishing. On the dish liquation was superimposed on the scrape marks, showing that overenthusiastic heating took place after scraping. The microsection shows no sign of surface working having taken place after the final heating process. Using a portable hardness tester, calibrated against a 70% gold-silver specimen (HV 85) readings were taken on the figures in the design (102 HV equivalent–average of about 10 readings in each case), the areas between the figures (83) and the back surface (98). A higher set of readings (average 110) was obtained on one of the figures near the centre. There seemed no obvious reason why this particular area should be harder, although the increased hardness might have been chance, it merited further consideration.

The effect of working a metal, whether by beating, chasing, scraping or burnishing is to increase its hardness. If the metal is then heated, annealing takes place, and the metal softens. The amount of softening relative to the worked hardness depends on the initial amount of work done, the temperature and time of annealing. The silver dish is by no means fully annealed (a hardness value of about 40–50 might then be expected), but neither is it fully hardened (sterling silver has a hardness value of 142 HV at 60% reduction in thickness which could be

extrapolated to give a value of roughly 125–130 for the hardened surface of the dish, which has a lower copper content and is intrinsically softer metal). It is clear from the hardness results and the microsections that heating which resulted in liquation on the back was the final process carried out on the dish. It seems unlikely that this occurred in antiquity: there would be no particular advantage unless further working was to be carried out and there would be a risk of spoiling the appearance of the dish, which has in fact happened. Liquation makes the surface look irregularly rough, and fire staining gives a slightly greyish coloration. The irregularity of the annealing, with one area remaining harder than the rest suggests that the application of heat was uneven, perhaps resulting from the use of a torch. There is no reason why the dish should have been heated with a torch finally in antiquity, but there is a good reason why it may have been done after excavation: corrosion is very easily removed in this way.

4 Soldering and the foot ring. According to Wolters[66] the Romans used 'the already traditional hard solders of gold-silver and silver-copper', but he quotes only the example of the Hildesheim silver hoard 'recently connected with the defeat of Varus in 9 AD'. Pliny (AD 23–79) reports the use of malachite as a reaction solder, and the granulation technique had been known and mastered for gold for some time, although used less frequently for silver. (Granulation is obtained where a copper salt mixed with glue holds the granules in place: on heating the copper salt goes to copper oxide, the glue to carbon; the carbon reduces the copper oxide to copper, which is then available to make a joint.) This technique is certainly more difficult to use for silver[67] and this may be why silver granulation is less frequently used. Maryon states that the Roman craftsmen were perfectly familiar with the process of hard soldering[68] and goes on to say that Pliny described it as it was practised by the craftsmen of his day. However, Pliny in fact describes gold soldering[69] using Cyprian copper verdigris and the urine of a boy, which are ground with soda in a copper mortar to produce a mixture referred to as Santerna. This was used for 'silvery gold', while 'coppery gold' was soldered using the same mixture with the addition of 'some gold and one seventh as much of silver'. In the next chapter Pliny says that 'the proper solder for silver should be stagnum', which is translated as stannum, a silver lead alloy (no proportions given). A modern silver lead alloy containing 97·5% lead, 1·5% silver + 1% tin, melting point 310 °C is used for coating and joining; other compositions have long soldification ranges and would be less satisfactory for joining.

There are in fact three places on the dish where soldering or brazing might have been used. These are (i) on the rim, where there are breaks, (ii) at the join of the rim and dish, and (iii) where the foot ring joins the dish.

(i) There are several breaks on the rim of the dish, where it looks as though soft soldering (i.e. with tin-lead) might have been used. However, neither spectrographic nor quantitative X-ray fluorescence analysis showed any signs of solder, tin was virtually absent while traces of lead were found, but in no greater quantity than were present elsewhere in the body of the dish. Nor was there an increased copper content to indicate that hard soldering had been employed. It is possible that an attempt was made to close the gaps by casting on a small quantity of molten silver. This would be a difficult operation because of the size of the dish which would rapidly cool the molten metal, probably before it had adequately wet the surfaces, and the residual stresses left in the rim of the dish would be sufficient to break the joint.

(ii) As indicated above, no trace of a join has been found where the beaded portion joins the dish, nor was there any sign of this where the vertical scraped rim joins the beaded section. It is concluded that they are all parts of the original piece of silver.

(iii) The foot ring was carefully examined to determine the means of attachment. It is possible that the foot ring was (a) part of the original casting, (b) that it was cast on, (c) soldered on with hard (silver-copper) solder, or attached by the granulation technique. There are no visible signs of solder and no change in colour is detectable at the joining point. Atomic absorption (ring only) and X-ray fluorescence analysis was carried out on the foot ring and the join, but the results do not show any significant differences between the foot ring, join area and dish. Examination showed small irregular

circumferential lines and cracks close to the ring, very firm scraping on the inner surface of the join, some signs of hammering so that on the base just inside the ring there is a series of faint radial corrugations which fade out somewhere near the traced line bounding the unscraped area at the centre. Radiography shows the metal of the ring and join to be very sound with no discontinuities, pin holes, cavities or flaws. Etches for silver and copper, which revealed soldered patches on the Water Newton vessels, did not show any areas of different composition at the join on the Neptune dish. The physical appearance of the join suggests either raising from a ring cast as part of the original or a soldered joint which has been considerably worked to make the surface even. The response to etching is consistent with casting or perhaps the use of the granulation techniques, the joining copper-rich layer this produces can only be resolved by high-power microscopy which could not be used at this location on the dish. Casting on seems unlikely in view of the complete soundness of the joint as shown by radiography. In view of the analysis results it seems most likely that the foot ring was part of the original casting.

It appears that soldering was not carried out on the dish, but an attempt to repair the rim was made by casting on a small amount of silver.

Conclusions
The dish was probably made much in the way that Maryon described, with the exception of the foot ring. The present examination suggested that the dish was cast as a thick disc with a rudimentary foot ring. It was raised to a suitable diameter and the rim thickened, probably by hammering. The foot ring was also raised. The design was executed entirely on the front face with punches and chasing tools, using the lateral displacement technique, while it was resting on a metal anvil. The edge of the dish was beaded and the rim turned down. Unsuccessful attempts to repair the breaks in the rim were made by casting on silver. The surfaces on the back, front, the rim and foot ring were scraped to smooth the surface, using a lathe. The figures and design on the front surface were burnished. Finally, the dish was flame annealed, probably after excavation, to remove corrosion products, and some surface melting took place.

Appendix B
Concordance of Registration Numbers with Painter and Brailsford Catalogue Numbers

Registration number	Painter Catalogue no.	Brailsford Catalogue no.	Painter Catalogue no.	Registration number	Brailsford Catalogue no.
1946.10-7.1	1	1	1	1946.10-7.1	1
1946.10-7.2	2	2	2	1946.10-7.2	2
1946.10-7.3	3	3	3	1946.10-7.3	3
1946.10-7.4	10	4	4	1946.10-7.11	5
1946.10-7.5	6	7	5	1946.10-7.12	6
1946.10-7.6	7	8	6	1946.10-7.5	7
1946.10-7.7	9	10	7	1946.10-7.6	8
1946.10-7.8	8	9	8	1946.10-7.8	9
1946.10-7.9	11	11	9	1946.10-7.7	10
1946.10-7.10	12	12	10	1946.10-7.4	4
1946.10-7.11	4	5	11	1946.10-7.9	11
1946.10-7.12	5	6	12	1946.10-7.10	12
1946.10-7.13	14	16	13	1946.10-7.15	13
1946.10-7.14	15	17	13	1946.10-7.16	14
1946.10-7.15	13	13	13	1946.10-7.17	15
1946.10-7.16	13	14	14	1946.10-7.13	16
1946.10-7.17	13	15	15	1946.10-7.14	17
1946.10-7.18	16	18	16	1946.10-7.18	18
1946.10-7.19	17	19	17	1946.10-7.19	19
1946.10-7.20	18	20	18	1946.10-7.20	20
1946.10-7.21	19	21	19	1946.10-7.21	21
1946.10-7.22	20	22	20	1946.10-7.22	22
1946.10-7.23	21	23	21	1946.10-7.23	23
1946.10-7.24	22	24	22	1946.10-7.24	24
1946.10-7.25	23	25	23	1946.10-7.25	25
1946.10-7.26	24	26	24	1946.10-7.26	26
1946.10-7.27	26	28	25	1946.10-7.28	27
1946.10-7.28	25	27	26	1946.10-7.27	28
1946.10-7.29	28	30	27	1946.10-7.31	29
1946.10-7.30	29	31	28	1946.10-7.29	30
1946.10-7.31	27	29	29	1946.10-7.30	31
1946.10-7.32	32	34	30	1946.10-7.34	32
1946.10-7.33	31	33	31	1946.10-7.33	33
1946.10-7.34	30	32	32	1946.10-7.32	34

Brailsford Catalogue no.	Registration number	Painter Catalogue no.
1	1946.10-7.1	1
2	1946.10-7.2	2
3	1946.10-7.3	3
4	1946.10-7.4	10
5	1946.10-7.11	4
6	1946.10-7.12	5
7	1946.10-7.5	6
8	1946.10-7.6	7
9	1946.10-7.8	8
10	1946.10-7.7	9
11	1946.10-7.9	11
12	1946.10-7.10	12
13	1946.10-7.15	13
14	1946.10-7.16	13
15	1946.10-7.17	13
16	1946.10-7.13	14
17	1946.10-7.14	15
18	1946.10-7.18	16
19	1946.10-7.19	17
20	1946.10-7.20	18
21	1946.10-7.21	19
22	1946.10-7.22	20
23	1946.10-7.23	21
24	1946.10-7.24	22
25	1946.10-7.25	23
26	1946.10-7.26	24
27	1946.10-7.28	25
28	1946.10-7.27	26
29	1946.10-7.31	27
30	1946.10-7.29	28
31	1946.10-7.30	29
32	1946.10-7.34	30
33	1946.10-7.33	31
34	1946.10-7.32	32

Notes

1. Conceşti: L. Matzulewitsch, *Byzantinische Antike*. Berlin, 1929, pls. 38, 40, 44-6. For a general discussion of 'picture dishes' see D. E. Strong, *Greek and Roman Gold and Silver Plate*. London, 1966, pp. 197-9.

2. D. E. Strong, op. cit., p. 194.

3. Traprain, no. 7: A. O. Curle, *The Treasure of Traprain. A Scottish Hoard of Roman Silver Plate*. Glasgow, 1923, pp. 25-6.

4. Parabiago: A. Levi, *La Patera di Parabiago* (Opera d'Arte, fasc. 5, 1935); Conceşti: L. Matzulewitsch, op. cit., note 1, above; Projecta casket (Esquiline Treasure): *British Museum Early Christian Catalogue*. London, 1901, no. 304; Corbridge lanx: Strong, op. cit., p. 198; Diana platter: H. Schlunk, *Kunst der Spätantike im Mittelmeerraum*. Berlin, 1939, pl. 29, p. 107; Baku dish: *Enciclopedia dell'Arte Classica*, s.v. Caucaso, and *Comptes Rendus de la Commission Impériale Archéologique* (1896), p. 114 and fig. 110.

5. J. M. C. Toynbee, *Art in Britain under the Romans*. Oxford, 1964, pp. 306-8. Professor Toynbee points out that the scene on the Corbridge lanx has been identified as a group of deities worshipped on the island of Delos. She argues convincingly that the Corbridge lanx is a pagan piece that depicts, not symbolic or allegorical mythology, but the recipients of cult at a temple. The appearance of such a scene at such a date can only be explained as a topical allusion to a specific event, namely to the sacrifice offered to Apollo on Delos by Julian the Apostate in AD 363, when he was *en route* for the Persian war. The lanx may therefore be dated to *c.* AD 363, and we may regard it as a memorial work, emanating from the circles of the pagan reaction.

6. E. Kitzinger, *Antiquity*, March 1940, pp. 43 ff.

7. A. O. Curle, *The Treasure of Traprain. A Scottish Hoard of Roman Silver Plate*. Glasgow, 1923.

8. O. M. Dalton, *Catalogue of the Early Christian Antiquities in the British Museum*. London, 1927. (Esquiline Treasure.)

9. E. H. Minns, *Scythians and Greeks*. Cambridge, 1913, p. 434; and Strong, op. cit., p. 195 and pl. 63A. This may date from about AD 300 and a pointillé inscription shows that it had come into the possession of the Bospotan King, Rhescuporis. Some of the plates in the Canoscio hoard are simply decorated with a niello cross or Chi-Rho monogram in the centre. Of the twenty-four silver vessels found at Canoscio in Umbria, which possibly all belonged to a Christian church, some are certainly as early as the fifth century AD: *Rivista di Archeologia Cristiana* xii (1935), pp. 313 ff., and E. Giovagnoli, *Il Tesoro Eucaristico di Canoscio*. Città di Castello, 1940.

10. R. Laur-Belart, *Der spätrömische Silberschatz von Kaiseraugst, Aargau*. Augst BL, 1963, no. 9, p. 24, and Abb. 13.

11. R. L. S. Bruce-Mitford, *The Sutton Hoo Ship Burial*, vol. 1. London, 1976, pp. 206-16; Conceşti, now in the Hermitage Museum, Leningrad: Matzulewitsch, *Byzantinische Antike: Studien auf Grund der Silbergefässe der Hermitage*. Berlin and Leipzig, 1929, pls. 36-43.

12. Cesena: *Annuario di R. Scuola Archaeologica di Atene* xxiv-xxvi (viii-x, 1946-8), pp. 309-44; Traprain: Curle, op. cit. (1923), pp. 56 ff.

13. Strong, op. cit., p. 194, quoting the

Lateran paintings (*Mem. Pont. Accad.* vii, 1944, p. 282, fig. 222), and the scenes shown on mosaics from Antioch (Glanville Downey, *Ancient Antioch.* Princeton, 1963, figs. 37 ff.).

14. H. B. Walters, *Catalogue of the Silver Plate, Greek, Etruscan and Roman, in the British Museum.* London, 1921, nos. 144–82.

15. The type of decoration can be matched on silver, bronze, and pottery vessels of the second to fourth centuries AD. On bronze vessels such decoration seems to be known only on the friezes of some of the so-called Hemmoor buckets—deep hemispherical bowls on a low foot with single or double bucket handles swivelling in vertical ring-attachments on opposite sides. Five examples of Hemmoor buckets are known in silver; but they are common in bronze between about AD 150 and 250; for silver: Strong, op. cit., pp. 160 ff.; bronze: M. H. P. Den Boestard, *The Bronze Vessels in the Rijksmuseum G. M. Kam at Nijmegen,* Leiden, 1956, pp. 44 ff.; pottery: J. W. Hayes, *Late Roman Pottery.* British School at Rome, 1972, pp. 283 ff. Drexel linked Hemmoor buckets with 'Alexandrian' silver plate and suggested a Pontic origin for the silver and bronze vessels and plate (Fr. Drexel, 'Alexandrinische Silbergefässe der Kaiserzeit', *Bonner Jahrbücher* 118, 1909, pp. 176–235); but Werner later demonstrated that the Hemmoor buckets and certain other types had a western distribution, and the buckets are now thought to have been made at Gressenich, near Aachen, and at Eisenberg in the Pfalz, near Heidelberg (J. Werner, *Bonner Jahrbücher* 140/1, 1936, pp. 395 ff; Gressenich: H. Willers, *Neue Untersuchungen über die römische Bronzeindustrie von Capua und von Niedergermanien.* Hannover and Leipzig, 1907, pp. 44–5, and A. Voigt, *Bonner Jahrbücher* 155/6, 1955–6, pp. 318 ff; Eisenberg: F. Sprater, *Das römische Eisenberg. Seine Eisen- und Bronzeindustrie.* Speyer, 1952). What still stands, however, is Drexel's suggestion that there are three main types of frieze found on cups, bowls, dishes and plates: (*a*) Dionysiac masks, animals, trees and buildings; (*b*) animals and hunters; and (*c*) fantastic sea-beasts, the smallest group. The types of frieze are linked by all three being found on those Hemmoor buckets which bear pictorial friezes, fifteen of the 124 known to Werner.

16. For a general discussion of the type see Strong, op. cit., pp. 201–2. Esquiline: Dalton, op. cit., no. 310; Traprain: Curle, op. cit., pp. 36–40, nos. 30, 31; Romania: E. C. Dodd, *Byzantine Silver Stamps.* Princeton, 1961, no. 84.

17. This bowl from Weiden is in Berlin: H. Schlunk, *Kunst der Spätantike im Mittelmeerraum.* Berlin, 1939, no. 103, pl. 27.

18. Traprain: Curle, op. cit., pp. 28–31.

19. Strong, op. cit., p. 153.

20. For the bases of jugs see Strong, op. cit., pp. 188–90.

21. Curle, op. cit., p. 30: Garrucci, *Storia della Arte Cristiana*, vol. vi, Tav. 418, no. 4.

22. J. W. Brailsford, *Guide to the Antiquities of Roman Britain.* London, 3rd ed., 1964, pp. 41–2.

23. For a discussion of ladles and the Mildenhall ladles in particular, Strong, op. cit., pp. 193–4. Carthage: O. M. Dalton, *Catalogue of the Early Christian Antiquities in the British Museum.* London, 1927, nos. 364–70; Canoscio and Desana: *Ori e Argenti dell'Italia Antica* (Exhibition in Turin, 1961), nos. 806–10; an unusual ladle, probably from Carthage, and now in the Louvre: A. de Ridder, *Musée National du Louvre, Catalogue Sommaire des Bijoux Antiques.* Paris, 1924, no. 1985.

24. Traprain: Curle, op. cit., no. 106.

25. E. C. Dodd, *Byzantine Silver Stamps.* Princeton, 1961.

26. Dodd, op. cit., no. 81: the stamp is rectangular with a figure of Tyche closely resembling that on a coin of Valentinian II (AD 383–392) and an inscription reading **ΑΒΑΛΑΤΟC CΦΡΑΓΙCΕΝ** ('Abalatos stamped it').

27. Dodd, op. cit., no. 83.

28. *Annuario di Scuola Archaeologica di Atene* xxiv–xxvi (viii–ix, 1946–8), pp. 309–44. The Cesena dish is the best-known example of the use of niello and gilding for figured scenes and is now in the Bibliotheca Malatestiana at Cesena.

29. The spoon now forms part of the collections of the Department of Prehistoric and Romano-British Antiquities; registration no. P.1971, 5-1, 1. K. S. Painter, 'A Roman Christian Silver Treasure from Biddulph, Staffordshire', *Antiquaries Journal* lv (1975), p. 62.

30. Canoscio Treasure: D. E. Giovagnoli, 'Una collezione di vasi eucaristici scoperti a Canoscio', *Rivista di Archeologia Cristiana* xii (1935), pp. 313–28. The spoon is illustrated in

fig. 7, p. 325 and is decorated in the bowl with a punched Chi-Rho and alpha and omega.

31. Carthage: O. M. Dalton, *Catalogue of Early Christian Antiquities and objects from the Christian East*. London, 1901, p. 81, no. 375. Hof Iben: Reinach, *Revue des Études Juives* 13 (1886), p. 220: F. X. Kraus, *Die altchristlichen Inschriften der Rheinlande*. Freiburg i. B., 1890, p. 24, no. 41; F. Cabrol and H. Leclerq, *Dictionnaire d'archeologie chrétienne et de liturgie III* (1914), 3175-6, s.v. 'cuiller'; Th. Kempf and W. Reusch (*eds.*), *Frühchristliche Zeugnisse im Einzugsgebiet von Rhein und Mosel*. Trier, 1965, p. 122, no. 111. Esquiline Treasure: Dalton, op. cit., no. 304. Coffin of Paulinus: Kempf and Reusch, op. cit., no. 53. Technique of inscription: it is of course possible that the Biddulph spoon was also inscribed in the first instance with short strokes and that they were afterwards obscured by a point which left a single line.

32. D. B. Harden, 'Late-Roman Wheel-Inscribed Glasses with Double-Line letters', *Kölner Jahrbuch* ix (1967-8), pp. 43-55. This builds on his earlier paper, 'The Highdown Hill Glass Goblet with Greek Inscription', *Sussex Archaeological Collections* 97 (1959), pp. 3-20. Dr Harden kindly informs me that yet other examples have come to his knowledge since he published his paper of 1967-8, but that the new information is in no way inconsistent with his previous conclusions.

33. On ingots and *largitio* dishes see K. S. Painter, 'A Late-Roman Silver Ingot from Kent', *Antiquaries Journal* lii (1972), pp. 84-92.

34. On centres of manufacture in the fourth and fifth centuries see Strong, op. cit., pp. 183-5.

35. For a basic discussion of the hoard see Toynbee, op. cit. (1964), pp. 308 ff.

36. Corbridge *lanx*: Toynbee, op. cit. (1964), pp. 306 ff.

37. Risley Park *lanx*: Strong, op. cit., pp. 185-6.

38. Curle, op. cit., pp. 28 ff., 36 ff. and 63 ff.

39. Curle, op. cit., pp. 36 ff.

40. Curle, op. cit., pp. 28 ff.

41. The 'Amiens Chalice' is thought in the light of recent work to be of the seventeenth century AD, together with its parallel pieces. See D. B. Harden, K. S. Painter, R. H. Pinder-Wilson and Hugh Tait, *Masterpieces of Glass*. London, 1968, no. 255. More apposite parallels for later two-handled cups are to be found in the third-century cup from Varpelev, Denmark, and the two elaborate multangular gold cups with animal handles in the fourth-century Treasure of Petrossa, from Romania (Strong, op. cit., pp. 165 and 188).

42. Curle, op. cit., pp. 63 ff.

43. For a recent and comprehensive study of late-Roman and Merovingian silver spoons see Vladimir Milojcic, 'Zu den spätkaiserzeitlichen und merowingischen Silberlöffeln', *49. Bericht der römisch-germanischen Kommission*, 1968 (Berlin, 1970), pp. 111-13. In his study of the spoon from Biddulph, Staffordshire, the present writer concludes: 'The uses of silver spoons in late Roman and early Christian times can be classified comparatively easily. Some are grave-offerings, a custom having its origins in heathen antiquity. Others are memorials, or good-luck offerings, for individuals, or at least apotropaic in their devices. Some are parts of table-services, while others appear in hoards of silver broken up for use as currency. A number had a Christian purpose with inscriptions or graffiti, like those on brooches or gravestones or other materials, which prayed that God might grant the named person a happy life now or hereafter. As far as the churches themselves were concerned, it should be remembered that in the Gallic church during the second Council of Orleans in AD 541, a church funeral feast was held, even though the custom had already been given up by the Italian church. In the Byzantine church up to the Council of Trulla in AD 692, it was the custom to hold a communal festival meal in the church itself, on Maundy Thursday, followed by communion. For any of these meals and particularly for some of the various forms of communion, silver spoons with pious inscriptions and dedications were clearly well suited. In contrast to the classification of uses, however, the attribution of any individual spoon to a particular use is impossible unless the circumstances and associations of its discovery are favourable and informative. It is obvious, moreover, that any such spoon can have had a multiplicity of uses either in succession or simultaneously.'

44. Strong, op. cit., pp. 185 ff., and Duchesne, *Liber Pontificalis* i, 79.

45. Canoscio: *Rivista di Archeologia Cristiana* xii, 1935, pp. 313 ff. E. Giovagnoli, *Il Tesoro Eucaristico di Canoscio*. Città di Castello, 1940.

For Christian ritual plate in general see W. F. Volbach, *Metallarbeiten des christlichen Kultus.* Mainz, 1921, and J. Braun, *Das christliche Altargeräte.* Munich, 1932.

46. On the conflict between paganism and Christianity in general see A. Momigliano (ed.), *The Conflict Between Paganism and Christianity in the Fourth Century.* Oxford, 1963, especially Chapter VIII, H. Bloch, 'The Pagan Revival in the West at the end of the Fourth Century'. It is particularly worth noting that under the later Empire bronze coins of Alexander the Great were used as charms (St John Chrysostom, *Ad illum catech* ii, 5 = Migne, Patr. Gr. xlix, 239); that people wore his portrait on their persons to bring them good luck, and that a toast was once drunk from a *patera 'quae in medio vultum Alexandri haberet et in circuitu omnem historiam contineret signis brevibus et minutulis'* (*Scriptores Historiae Augustae, Tyranni Triginta*, 14, 2-6). Portraits of Alexander and Olympias and scenes from the King's career would thus be appropriate on the contorniates—and on silver plate—as auguring good luck, as would pictures of gods such as Jupiter, the Dioscuri, Hercules, Bacchus, Apollo, Sol, Mars, Vulcan, Minerva, Diana, Cybele, etc. At this point it is also worth drawing attention to the themes of the Treasure of Pietroasa—particularly those on the splendid gold dish which relate to this pantheon—which may well have been deposited about AD 381 (Ecaterina Dunareanu-Vulpe, *Le Trésor de Pietroasa*, Editions Meridiane, Bucarest, 1967).

47. A. Alföldi, *Die Kontorniaten. Ein verkanntes Propagandamittel der stadtrömischen heidnischen Aristokratie in ihrem Kampfe gegen das christliche Kaisertum.* Budapest, 1943. Alföldi suggests that the contorniates may have been New Year's gifts distributed as pagan propaganda by the pagan aristocracy of Rome.

48. Toynbee, *Journal of Roman Studies* xxxv (1945), pp. 115-21, has suggested that the contorniates 'may have been mementoes distributed to people at the beginning of every show'.

49. Ammianus Marcellinus xvi, 10, 13 ff., and xvii, 4. See also Toynbee, 'An Imperial Institute of Archaeology as Revealed by Roman Medallions', *Archaeological Journal* xcix (1943), pp. 33-47, especially p. 47.

50. Dessau, *Inscriptiones Latinae Selectae*, 736.

51. A. H. M. Jones, *The Later Roman Empire, 284-602*. Oxford, 1964, vol. i, pp. 120 ff.

52. Sir Ellis Minns quoted as a close analogy for the letter-forms a papyrus of AD 314: Schubart *Pap. Graec. Ber.*, pl. 38a.

53. This was first pointed out to J. W. Brailsford by Mr T. C. Skeat, formerly Keeper of the Department of Manuscripts: Ammianus Marcellinus, xvi, 7.

54. For details of both types of hoards and detailed references see Strong, op. cit., pp. 182 ff.

55. R. Laur-Belart, *Der spätrömische Silberschatz von Kaiseraugst, Aargau.* Augst BL, 1963, pp. 3-5. The argument is supported by the coins, which are likely to have been buried between about AD 350 and 360.

56. Ammianus Marcellinus xx, 4: Julian is summoned from Gaul by Constantius II to meet the Persian threat. Ammianus xxv, 3: Julian dies in conflict with the Persians.

57. For the troubles of this period in general and particular see S. S. Frere, *Britannia, A History of Roman Britain.* London, 1967 (3rd impression, 1969), pp. 349 ff.

58. Ammianus Marcellinus xx, 1, 1 ff.

59. Ammianus Marcellinus, xx, 1; Ammianus Marcellinus, xx, 9, 9: *et quoniam cum haec ita procederent, timebatur Lupicinus, licet absens agensque etiam tum apud Britannos, homo superbae mentis et turgidae, eratque suspicio quod (si haec trans mare didicisset) novarum rerum materias excitaret, notarius Bononiam mittitur, observaturus sollicite, ne quisquam fretum oceani transire permitteretur. quo vetito, reversus Lupicinus antequam horum quicquam sciret, nullas ciere potuit turbas.*

60. Julian, *Letter to the Athenians*, 281-2.

61. Lupicinus' Christianity: Theodoret, Bishop of Cyrrhus (c. AD 393-466), *Religiosa Historia* 13 = Migne, Patrologiae Cursus, series Graeca, columns 1407-8: 82. Paris, 1859, ch. 1213. The text is given by Migne in Latin and in Greek. The Latin text is as follows: *Cum autem vitam ageret in monte, pastor quidam, palantes quaerens oves, ad locum pervenit, in quo erat vir Dei. Obscura porro nox erat, et nix multa descenderat: viditque, ut referebat, pyram circa ipsum accensam, et duos alba veste indutos, qui materiam igni subministrarent. Quippe animi alacritatem afferens, divina ope fruebatur. Sed et prophetici quoque doni particeps fuit. Cum enim ad eum venisset magister militum, religione illustris (Lupicini enim virtutem quis nescit?), sollicitumque se esse diceret de quibusdam, qui ab urbe regia res*

sibi necessarias mari advehebant; quinquaginta namque aiebat elapsos dies esse, cum ex portu solvissent, nec de illis ad se famam ullam pervenisse, ille nihil cunctatus: 'Navis, inquit, amice, una periit. altera Seleuciae portum craes intrabit.' Et haec quidem divino illo ex ore audivit, verborum autem veritatem experientia perdidicit.

62. If the Corbridge *lanx* is correctly assigned to AD 363, the hiding of it and its associated pieces, now lost, is presumably to be attributed to one of the subsequent barbarian crises associated with the *barbarica conspiratio*, perhaps in AD 365 or 367.

63. Herbert Maryon, 'The Mildenhall Treasure: some technical problems', Part I, *Man*, March, 1948, pp. 25-7; Part II, *Man*, April, 1948, pp. 38-41.

64. Pliny, *Natural History*, Book XXXIII, ch. xlix: *vasa ex argento mire inconstantia humani ingenii variat nullum genus officinae diu probando. nunc Furniana, nunc Clodiana, nunc Gratiana—etenim tabernas mensis adoptamus— nunc anaglypta asperitatemque exciso circa liniarum picturas quaerimus, iam vero et mensas repositoriis inponimus ad sustinenda opsonia, interradimus alia, ut quam plurimum lima perdiderit.*

65. Alfred Mutz, *Die Kunst des Metalldrehens bei den Römern* (Basel and Stuttgart, 1972).

66. Jochen Wolters, *On the History of Soldering* (Degussa, 1975).

67. C. J. Wheatley, unpublished work.

68. H. Maryon, *Man*, April, 1948, p. 41.

69. Pliny, *Natural History*, Book XXXIII, ch. xxix. The full text reads: *chrysocollam et aurifices sibi vindicant adglutinando auro, et inde omnes appellatas similiter virentes dicunt. temperatur autem Cypria aerugine et pueri inpubis urina addito nitro teriturque Cyprio vocant nostri. ita feruminatur aurum, quod argentosum vocant. signum est, si addita santerna intescit. e diverso aerosum contrahit se hebetaturque et difficultur feruminatur ad id glutinum fit auro et septima argenti parte ad supra dicta additis unaque tritis.*

Select Bibliography

An exhaustive bibliography on the Mildenhall Treasure would be inappropriate in a publication of this kind. Numerous references will, however, be found in the notes to the main text, while the brief bibliography below gives some major references of general interest, including the only publications up to the present in which the treasure has been catalogued in detail.

J. W. BRAILSFORD, *The Mildenhall Treasure*. London, 1947, reprinted 1964.

T. DOHRN, 'Spätantikes Silber aus Britannien', *Mitteilungen des deutschen archäologischen Instituts* ii (1949), p. 67.

J. M. C. TOYNBEE, *Art in Roman Britain*. London, 1962, pp. 169-71, pls. 113-19, 124.

J. M. C. TOYNBEE, *Art in Britain under the Romans*. Oxford, 1964, pp. 308-12.

D. E. STRONG, *Greek and Roman Gold and Silver Plate*. London, 1966, esp. pp. 182 ff.

K. S. PAINTER, 'The Mildenhall Treasure: a Reconsideration', *British Museum Quarterly* xxxvii (1973), pp. 154 ff.

The Plates

2 The Great Dish; detail of centre, with the head of Oceanus

3 The Great Dish; detail of inner frieze, with sea-creatures and Nereids

4 The Great Dish; detail from the outer frieze, showing Bacchus, Silenus, a dancing satyr, and a Maenad

5 The Great Dish; detail from the outer frieze with the drunken Hercules supported by satyrs

6 The Great Dish; detail from the outer frieze showing Pan and a dancing Maenad

7 The Bacchic platters. *Catalogue no. 2* (left), and *no. 3* (right)

8 Platter; detail of Maenad. *Catalogue no. 3*

9 Platter; graffito, ευθηριου, under base. *Catalogue no. 3*

11 The niello dish; detail of centre decoration

12-14 The niello dish; details of rim decoration

15 Flanged bowls. *Catalogue no.* 6 (left), and *no.* 5 (right)

16 Flanged bowl; detail of centre medallion. *Catalogue no.* 5

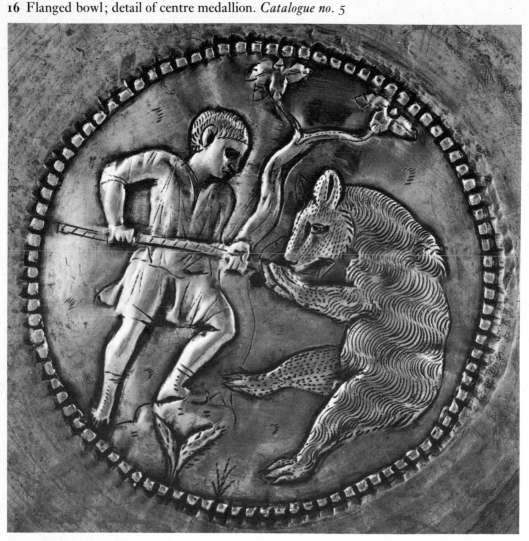

17 Flanged bowl; inscriptions on underside of flange. *Catalogue no.* 5

18 Flanged bowl; detail of centre medallion. *Catalogue no. 6*

19 Flanged bowl; dotted inscription on the underside of the flange. *Catalogue no. 6*

20 Flanged bowls. *Catalogue no. 8* (left), and *no. 7* (right)

Flanged bowl; centre detail, with head of Olympias. *Catalogue no. 8*

22 Flanged bowl; detail of centre medallion, with head of Alexander the Great.
Catalogue no. 7

23 Pair of flanged bowls. *Catalogue no. 9* (left), and *no. 10* (right)

24 Flanged bowl; detail of rim. *Catalogue no.* 9

25 Flanged bowl; detail of rim. *Catalogue no. 10*

26 Bowl with cover. *Catalogue nos. 11 and 12*

27 Bowl with cover

28 Bowl with cover; detail of decoration

29 Pair of goblets. *Catalogue nos. 13 and 14*

30 Pair of goblets; decoration beneath the bases

31 Fluted bowl with handles. *Catalogue nos. 15-17*

32 Fluted bowl with handles

33 Ladles with dolphin handles. *Catalogue nos. 18–26*

34 Ladle with dolphin handle; detail to show modelling of dolphin

35 Spoons with inscriptions. *Catalogue no. 28* (upper), and *no. 27* (lower)

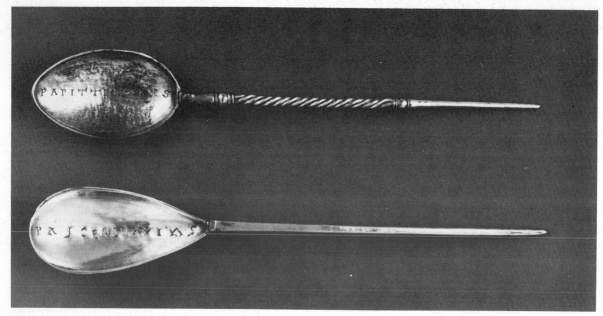

36 Three spoons with Chi-Rho monograms. *Catalogue no. 30* (upper), *no. 31* (middle), and *no. 29* (lower)

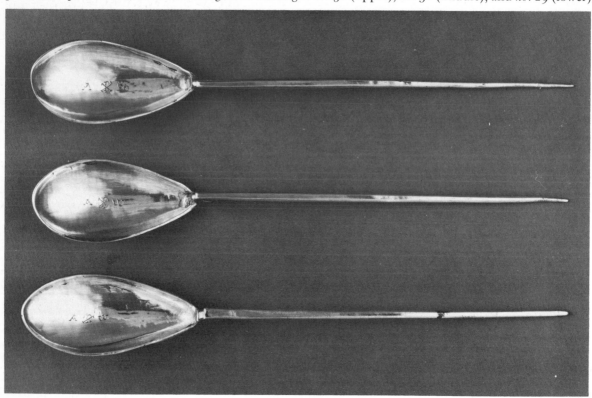

37 Three decorated spoons. *Catalogue no. 32* (upper), *no. 34* (middle), and *no. 33* (lower)